ORATORE:

THE ART OF
COMMUNICATION

ORATORE:

THE ART OF
COMMUNICATION

Matt Eventoff

King George Media Group, 3030 Olive Street, Dallas, Texas 75219
For email requests, please contact the publisher at info@kinggeorgemedia.com

ISBN-13: 978-1496127228
ISBN-10: 1496127226

Editor: Ailsa Campbell
Cover design and text composition: Clark Kenyon
www.camppope.com

Princeton
Public Speaking

Acknowledgments

To the greatest, most supportive, wife, mother, father, sister, "brothers" and family a man could ever ask for.

To my mentors, who have helped me grow every step of the way.

To my mentees, friends and clients around the world who I am fortunate to learn from every day.

And to the next generation of orators who will change the world through communication.

Thank you.

Table of Contents

Introduction

IF YOU'VE EVER faced an audience with sweaty palms, wondered how to become a better communicator during meetings, or struggled with putting your best foot forward in an interview, this book was created for you.

Here you will find wisdom gleaned from famous orators of the past together with tips on how to handle communicating in today's fast paced and technologically advanced world. This book will provide you with a comprehensive guide to creating dynamic presentations no matter what setting or situation.

From the boardroom to the classroom or even along the campaign trail: the tips, techniques, and tools Matt has gathered here represent key public speaking and communication lessons that are sure to enhance all of your interactions.

CHAPTER 1

CREATING AN EFFECTIVE PRESENTATION

CHAPTER 1

CREATING AN EFFECTIVE PRESENTATION

Strategies for Opening a Presentation

The audience is seated. The lights dim and the room quiets. All eyes are on the dais, waiting for the presentation to begin. All too often, this is what is heard to open the speech or presentation:

> "Hi, thank you for having me. It is an honor to be here with you today. My name is _____, and I am going to be speaking to you today about _____."

Looking around, here is what we tend to see:

- People reviewing a physical copy of the program, their previous notes, or additional handouts.

- T-U-T/T-O-T – Typing under table/typing on table. The smartphones are out in full force. It is not unusual to see people utilizing laptops, netbooks, or tablets.

- Eyes looking up. Eyes looking down.

- Eyes looking everywhere but at the speaker.

With all of this going on, how do you effectively open a speech or presentation? Here are a number of effective ways:

1) **Quote** – Name any topic and, more often than not, there is a great quote or saying that suits your subject matter perfectly. Here is an example of a quote that I often use to open a presentation dealing with public speaking:

> "It usually takes me more than three weeks to prepare a good impromptu speech." – Mark Twain

2) **What If** – Using a "what if…" scenario to draw your audience into your presentation is important, and doing so early on can work wonders. Encourage your audience to get involved right away by painting a scenario.

3) **Imagine** – This follows the same thought process as "what if." Put your audience members directly into the presentation by allowing each member to visualize a scenario.

4) **Question** – Rhetorical or literal – when someone is presented with a question (whether an answer is called for or not) that person intuitively answers it, even if it's just in his or her mind… and now that person is involved.

5) **Power Word** – Again, the emphasis is on choosing a word or phrase that is compelling.

> "Conflict" (long pause)
> "Never again" (long pause)

6) **Triads** – (Friends, Romans, countrymen; Students, Parents, Alumni; Employees, Management, Ownership.)

7) **Repetition** – (I will not, I will not, I will not… give up.)

8) **Statement** – A powerful statement, left to hang (followed by a pause), can be very effective. Inspirational political speeches and locker room speeches often start this way.

14

"We cannot win. We can't win."
(Pause)
"That's what every newspaper in the country is saying..."

9) **Silence** – Yes, silence! A pause, whether 2 seconds or 20 seconds, allows your audience to sit and quiet down. Most audiences expect a speaker to begin immediately. But, an extra pause brings all attention right where you want it – on you!

10) **Statistic** – Don't use a boring or complicated statistic; focus instead on a surprisingly powerful or personalized statistic.

> "Look to your left. Now look to your right. One of your seatmates will _____."
> "In this room, over 90 percent of us are going to _____."
> "The size of _____ football fields..."
> "The size of New York and Belgium combined..."
> "Picture a_____."

11) **Story** – We tell stories every single day. However, it is only when we think consciously about it that our minds go blank. Here are two easy templates to help create a story quickly:

> WWWCR:
> Who
> What
> Where
> Conflict
> Resolution
> *Or:*
> Triple C:
> Character
> Conflict
> (The) Comeback

12) **Simile** – X and Y are compared – using "like" or "as".

> Examples:
> • As blind as a bat.

- To work like a dog.

- As strong as an ox.

13) **Metaphor** – Applying X to Y when it is not literally applicable.

   Examples:
   - Has a heart of gold.

   - Food for thought.

   - Time is money.

14) **Current Event – Pick up a** *USA Today* **a few days before (ideas galore).**

15) **Moment in Time** – Just yesterday, last week, etc.

16) **Provocative Statement** – Say something that is attention-grabbing.

17) **Analogies** – Just as a sword is the weapon of a warrior, a pen is the weapon of a writer.

18) **Five Senses** – It felt like… It smelled like… It looked like… It sounded like… It tasted like…. (E.g. home-baked chocolate cookies convey warmth; smell of lemon is clean; warm lavender walls give a sense of calm.) – Using visual language, incorporating other senses to set the scene.

19) **Illustrations** – "Picture a _____. It was a perfect summer day…salt in the ear, the sounds of seagulls and waves crashing; The ocean was a pallid blue." Paint a verbal picture.

20) **Rhetorical Devices** – Basic list available in Chapter 8.

21) **Activity** – Get them active – get them to do something! Get up. Move. Write something down. Shake hands with the person next to them. Or greet the person behind them. Repeat something to them…

Learning is accentuated when someone needs actually to do

something, so a neat way to incorporate that into a speech is to say – 'Repeat after me" – or have them draw something in the air: "Take your index finger and draw a man." This helps retention!

22) **Prop** – can be used to illustrate a point or begin a story.

23) **Promise** – "By the end of this presentation, I guarantee that_____"
"If we go and do _____, I can promise that_____."

Tips on Closing a Presentation

The moment of truth has arrived. You have had them entranced from the start. The audience has been clearly focused, nodding as you delivered your message; eyes locked as you wove through a carefully crafted medley of stories, anecdotes, and analogies – all supporting your mission.

There is no question that the majority of your audience probably agree with what you are saying. Now empowered, the time has come for you to conclude, at which point you exclaim:

"In conclusion, I appreciate you giving your time to hear about _____. Thank you."

And then nothing happens. Everyone quietly claps or just nods, and then leaves the auditorium or conference room.

What happened? What can you do to prevent this from occurring? Each of the 20+ tips listed for opening a presentation can also work for closing. However, to try something different, here are five tried-and-true techniques for closing a presentation:

1) **Offer a Direct Call-to-Action:** A speech or presentation without a clear call-to-action is one that is probably not worth giving. While it may not be appropriate for every speech, there is no clearer call-to-action than a direct call-to-action.

"In order to guarantee that we save _____ tomorrow,

we need to _____ today. If every person in this room leaves and immediately _____, I can guarantee it will result in _____ next year!"

2) **(Very) Short Story/Anecdote:** Show, don't tell! Use a brief story or anecdote to drive a message home. I once had a Major League Baseball player as a client and he very effectively told the following (abridged) story to end a presentation about teamwork:

> "So Coach entered the locker room after a pretty tough game in which a number of us had standout performances, and the result was....a big loss. One of our players went four for four. Coach called him by his last name, Smith, asked him to come up front, and then asked him to stand with the back of his uniform facing the rest of the players. Then he asked a kid who had just been called up from the minors, Jones, to do the same thing. He then said, 'Smith, Jones, I want you to turn around.' When they did, he pointed to the front of the uniform and reminded us all – 'You play for the name on the front of the jersey (the team) not the name on the back (your own).'"

3) **Call-to-Question:** It is often very effective to end a presentation or speech with a rhetorical question that captures the message and leaves the audience thinking – especially one that directly ties in a call-to-action:

> "What choice will you make when you leave here today? Will you _____ or will you go about your normal routine?"

4) **Contrast:** One of my favorites! This one is even more effective when tied directly to the closing call-to-action:

> "We can have _____ or we can have _____. The choice is ours, and is based entirely on the decision we each individually make today. _____ or _____. I know I'm choosing _____."

5) **Quote:** Short, appropriate, and powerful quotes are effective for

both opening and closing a speech or presentation. There is a plethora of resources available online to find good quotes.

6) **Callback:** Most common; "Earlier today..."; "As we discussed at the beginning..." "Tying everything together...."

7) **Steve Jobs Close:** One More Thing – "One more thing... In the immortal words of Steve Jobs...."

8) **Return to Open:** "I asked you in the beginning...."; "_____ (a famous author) once wrote that..."

9) **Repetition:** Repeating earlier key phrase, and silence (bowed head)...then.... "Thank you."

10) **Powerful phrase:** "Be kind."

11) **Activity:** Get them active – get them to do something! Get up. Move. Write something down. Shake hands with the person next to them. Or behind them. Repeat something to them...

12) **Lyrics:** Song lyrics that are powerful:

> "I'm starting with the man in the mirror, I'm asking him to change his ways. And no message could have been any clearer. If you want to make the world a better place take a look at yourself and make a change."
> "Man in the Mirror" by Michael Jackson

> "If you've lost your way
> I will keep you safe."
> Westlife

13) **Quiet:** Notice how Broadway shows end – with silence. Concerts. The spotlight comes on... or just quiet, and then after a long pause..."Thank you."

14) **Excerpts from Literature: I** happen to favor Steinbeck (especially *Grapes of Wrath*).

Tom Joad: "Wherever you can look – wherever there's a fight, so hungry people can eat, I'll be there. Wherever there's a cop beatin' up a guy, I'll be there."

15) **Promise:** See above (under Open).

Examples of Presentation Structures

Classic Structure

- Open.
- Message.
- Three Supporting Points (with transitions).
- Close.

Solution Structure

- Open – Frame the Problem:
- Fact: "9 in 10 Americans don't know…"
- A few points about why it matters.
- Solve the Problem – Close.

Debate Structure (Tricky but Effective)

- Open.
- Frame the issue.
- Give each argument against your point (without prejudice).
- Finish with your solution (after all other options have been exhausted).
- Call-to-action.

Three Act Structure (Think Movies)

- Setup – set the stage.

- Confrontation – can be internal; does not have to be between individuals.
- Resolution.

Other structures

- Chronological – most common.
- Demonstrative – think Steve Jobs.
- Question and Answer – ask, then answer, your own questions.
- Story Structure – Steve Jobs's Stanford Speech – Open, Message, Stories (1-3) which support that message, close.

Professor Monroe's Motivating Sequence

- Attention – Grab attention – Open.
- Need – Demonstrate problem or need.
- Satisfaction – Propose your solution.
- Visualization – WIIFA (What's In It For the Audience).
- Action – Prompt to take action – Problem/solution.

Persuasive Speech – The 10 S © Formula

- Start Strong – the Open.
- State It – Key Message/Position/Theme.
- Shift – Transition.
- First "Message Support."
- Shift – Transition.
- Second "Message Support."
- Shift – Transition.
- Third "Message Support."
- Shift – Transition.
- Seek Support – Call-to-Action.

Structure for Longer Presentations (Hint...it's the same!)

- Open – Start Strong.
- State It – Key Message/Position/Theme.

Now, think of each support as its own mini-presentation, with a brief open and close, and a break for a few seconds in between to allow the audience to digest and re-engage; I tend to prefer utilizing questions as a tool to open these mini-modules, answer with the support, and close by reinforcing the support and/or transitioning.

- Support 1 – Open, Support, Close.
- Support 2 – Open, Support, Close.
- Support 3 – Open, Support, Close.
- Seek Support – Close the entire presentation.

Impromptu/Caught Off Guard/No Time to Prepare Speech

- Honoring Someone/Toasting/Etc. (PPF)
- Past – "I have known _____ for...."
- Present – "Today, I am thrilled to see_____..."
- Future – "Wishing _____ a world of happiness..."

Presentation

1) Question – "Why does ABC need to worry about DEF?"

   Answer/Message – "DEF keeps me up at night because ....."
   Quote – "Let's follow the counsel of ___, when she stated ...."

2) Ask yourself the Big 3, and then answer:

   a) "If you only remember one thing that I tell you, I want you to remember...."
   b) "This is why _____ matters to you..."
   c) "This is what you can do about it..."

3) Answer the traditional – who, what, when, where, why, and how – again; start by asking and answering your own question.

4) Make it personal – address any experience you have had with the topic at hand; if you have no experience, transition by comparing it to a situation you are familiar with.

What is Your Message?

According to Merriam-Webster Dictionary... a message is an underlying theme or idea.

Every organization has a message. Unfortunately, it usually goes undiscovered. If you try to communicate too many things, you end up communicating nothing. So how do we develop a message that anyone and everyone can understand? The following tips can help.

First and foremost, an effective message should contain the characteristics of the Eventoff matrix, given below.

Eventoff Messaging Matrix™

The "6 R" Messaging Method

Every message should be:

> Riveting – *can it capture attention?*
> Relevant – *does it matter to the audience?*
> Relatable – *can one relate based on previous experience?*
> Retainable – *is it impactful enough to have staying power?*
> Repeatable – *is it memorable and easy to repeat?*
> Reactionable – *is there something to do, or some way to react?*

1) Ask yourself the **first four questions**.

What are you trying to accomplish?

Who is your audience?

What is the one thing that they absolutely need to know?

Why does your audience care?

2) Then... **focus** in on two questions – What + Why.

What – If my audience forgets everything and can only remember one thing that I say, what should that be?

Why – Why *should* my audience care?

3) Next... provide **three supporting reasons**.

4) Under each reason – **substantiate and support.**

- Simple Stories
- Facts
- Figures
- Quotes
- Statistics
- Contrasts
- Questions (rhetorical or literal)
- Metaphors (something is something) – "All the world's a stage."
- Similes (something is like something; something is as something) – "Strong as an ox."
- Anecdotes
- Analogies
- Comparisons
- Contrasts (contrasting pairs)
- Testimonials
- Literature
- Social Proof
- Research
- Studies
- Opinion
- Media Coverage
- Historical Precedent
- Market Success
- Industry Measures
- "Standard of Care"

- Examples

5) Then... ask the **final question**.

    What do you want them to do?

6) Finally... plug into the **10S Template**.

    Start Strong – the Open
    State It – Key Message/Position/Theme
    (Question 2)
    Shift – Transition
    First "Message Support"
    Shift – Transition
    Second "Message Support"
    Shift – Transition
    Third "Message Support"
    Shift —Transition
    Seek Support – Call-to-Action
    (Question 5.)

An Example of the 10S Structure:

Open – Start Strong
"Be Sincere. Be Brief. Be Seated." – President Franklin D. Roosevelt

Message – State It (What + Why = Message)
"Brevity is the key to effective communication, and the key to more compelling presentations."

Transition – Shift
"Why is brevity so important?"

Support #1 – Statistic
Lloyd's Attention Span Study

Dr. Medina Research

Transition – Shift
"Now that we have looked at attention span, let's take a look at history."

Support #2 – Fact; Anecdote
Lincoln's Gettysburg Address – 272 words (200 one syllable words; under 3 minutes).

Edwin Everett's Address – 13,000+ words (over 2 hours).

Transition – Shift
"Now, please ask yourself, when was the last time you watched a presentation and said, 'Wow, I wish that went on for another 30 minutes!'"

Support #3 – Example; Experience
"Having watched thousands of speeches and presentations, when I overhear people talking during breaks, very, very rarely does anyone talk about the 'riveting past hour.'

"This is not a new concept – Cicero (107–43 B.C.), the famous Roman orator (amongst many other professions) stated: 'Brevity is the best recommendation in speech, in senator or in orator.'

"There is a misconception that forcing TMI (too much information) and CUA (constant useless acronyms) on an audience is necessary. Remember, if your audience doesn't follow you, or loses interest, who did you actually influence, persuade or move?"

Transition – Shift
"So which model of speech will you follow?"

Seek Support – Close
"The question really is: who is your presentation designed for, and whose interest is paramount: the presenter's, or the audience's?"

Tips on Transitions

Here you will find some ways to transition between "message supports" and "thoughts" within your presentation.

- Questions – A favorite. "So why would we _____? We would _____ because _____."
- Chronological – "First…"
- Markers – "We established earlier. Remember…"
- Itemize – "Three points… a) _____ b) _____ c) _____"
- Physical – "Now let's look at…" "We've covered…"
- Adverbs – While, Often, Recently, Now
- Phrases – "Let's look at…"

CHAPTER 2

PREPARING FOR A PRESENTATION

CHAPTER 2

PREPARING FOR A PRESENTATION

"Focus" Your Presentation

Focus groups have long been the domain of political campaigns. Focus groups can be used to test messages, appearances, images, sound bites, and oppositional research, etc. Focus groups have since become a staple in the corporate world, where products, messages, slogans, ad campaigns, and competition are regularly tested.

Litigators effectively utilize focus groups to test key messages. So do candidates for office. I find that the true value of a focus group is not necessarily to discover why a candidate or product is well liked, but rather, why they aren't liked. For example, "This is what we do not like about your message or argument." This information can be used to improve a product or change minds.

I am a believer that every person, whether a front line associate or CEO, can benefit from running a mini focus group prior to a high stakes speech, investor pitch, or presentation. Again, this is not to validate how "good" your presentation is, but to see where there are soft spots, weaknesses, and areas for improvement. Here are a few steps to set up a quick, effective focus group before your next big speech:

1) **Know your audience** – Who will be represented in the audience? Employees? Board Members? Investors? Have a representative in your focus group from each of the various sectors that will be represented in the audience. The group does not have to be big, nor does it have to be formal – it just has to be representative.

2) **Friends are not always your friends** – When running focus groups for litigators, I shy away from having a firm member participate as a focus group member. What you are looking for is distance from the issue. People that you know, respect, and trust – but do not necessarily spend all of your time with – often offer the best feedback.

3) **Friends are not always your friends, Pt. II** – For this reason, I also try to avoid having people participate who are very close to each other. It tends to skew the dynamic and often overpowers the group, leading to missing key feedback.

4) **Preparation** – I like to throw just about everything that I am planning on speaking about out there. Sometimes I am just too close to the topic and miss things that might be more effective or beneficial to my audience. An unprepared speech or presentation will focus all of the attention on delivery and not much on the message – meaning that you will get half of the value. Spend some time preparing.

5) **Ask!** – If you are a front-line associate, ask your mentor to sit in to represent executives. Conversely, C-level executives often balk at having a lower-level associate watch a presentation first. There is undoubtedly some risk, but I have done it a number of times and it has worked every time. The key is to identify the right person to participate. You are looking for a very small group. Again, not to validate how "good" you are, but to offer new opinions and bring a different perspective.

Prepare Like an NBA All Star

800 "makes."

A trainer hired to help Team USA prepare for the Olympics recalled his experience working with Laker legend Kobe Bryant. Bryant woke up his trainer to begin practicing, on his own, at 4a.m., and didn't conclude until seven hours later, after conditioning, weight work, and making 800 shots. *He had to be done because at 11a.m. he had a scrimmage with other Olympic (NBA) all-stars!*

So what does an NBA legend have to do with public speaking? Here is one of the greatest athletes in the world, and he is still practicing for seven hours, with intention, prior to a scrimmage.

I am constantly asked to share the "secrets" to effective public speaking. The reply is simple, and is no secret: practice and preparation. Practice and preparation are simple in concept, but not easy. They are also integral to the success of any presentation. There are also no bigger factors in helping ease anxiety and nerves prior to presenting than practice and preparation.

I present a few times every week, and I practice a presentation a minimum of seven times (usually more) before I actually present. Every single time.

I begin the preparation phase knowing that the presentation will take on numerous iterations prior to being delivered. That is the beauty of the process – seeing what works, and what doesn't. Initially, during the preparation phase I focus on:

1) Determining what my core message is;
2) How to support that message;
3) How to open with impact;
4) How to transition between supports;
5) How to include my audience; and finally;
6) How to close with power and move my audience to act.

Practice Like a Professional

I then move to the next phase, which is beginning to practice. I work with an outline for the initial practice session, to determine how I might want to transition, how to interact with the audience, what works, and what doesn't. There are a number of ways every person reading this can do the same.

Here are six tips:

1) **Determine your Message** – as well as your key supporting points. Determine what your message is, what the one thing that you need every member of the audience to remember is, and why your audience should care. This has to happen prior to practicing (although the practice process will help root this as well.)

2) **Power of Video** – Nearly everyone has a smartphone. Set it on the counter, and tape yourself. While this is not particularly enjoyable, it is revealing, and will help you to determine what is working, and what is not working.

3) **Find a Friend** – Practice in front of audiences who may or may not know anything about the subject matter. This (a) ramps up the pressure a bit and (b) provides great feedback as to the power of the message, and the delivery of that message.

4) **Back to the Camera** – Refinement time. At this point the presentation, or your portion of it, has really begun to take shape. This is where your 800 "makes" come into play. Tape yourself again – look at your movement, get a feel for your cadence, and lend a sharper ear to your vocal qualities (pitch, rate, inflection, tone, projection, etc.)

5) **Advanced** – "Mime Work" – To work on non-verbal delivery, and to really "feel" what I am expressing, I will actually practice, on tape, delivering the presentation without words. My mouth won't open. My puppy gets very confused, and I might look a bit

odd, but the results are telling, as I am able to focus not only on posture and gesturing, but on facial movements and expressions as well.

6) **Stop** – My goal with preparation, and practice, is not to be scripted, but to be so comfortable with my message, and myself, that I can be totally present on presentation day. On presentation day, I will only practice my open, as at this point the message is already "in my DNA." I will focus on relaxing and working through strategies to help deal with any anxiety I might be facing. Here is a great resource for handling anxiety and fear.

I believe that with practice and preparation, every person can be a successful presenter. Every person. But how many people will put the time in?

Ask yourself how many legends, in any field, succeed without practice. Then start preparing for your next meeting or presentation!

CHAPTER 3

DURING A PRESENTATION

CHAPTER 3

DURING A PRESENTATION

Audience Participation

In any presentation, one of the keys to audience participation is to establish a connection with members of the audience.

I firmly believe that you can establish a connection before you even begin to present formally!

A presentation can begin before an individual takes the stage or reaches the front of the room. A presentation begins the first time an audience member encounters the speaker. And this can be used to your benefit the next time you speak.

So how can you establish this connection prior to the presentation and the participation that follows?

Introduce yourself before your presentation is scheduled to begin.

"Hi, I'm Matt Eventoff, it is a pleasure to meet you."

Whether speaking to 30 or 300 people, I try to arrive as early as possible and position myself at the entrance of the room where I am presenting and introduce myself. If that isn't possible, and I am already in the room, I try to meet the few people surrounding me. This changes the mood in the room immediately, as now I am no longer speaking to a room full of strangers. There are now at least a few friendly faces, and a few folks who I can count on to participate. And participation typically begets participation.

Learning During Presentations

There has been much research done on how different individuals learn. Personally, I believe in incorporating "something for everyone" into each presentation. This can be accomplished by appealing to the three learning styles you encounter most often – visual, auditory, and kinesthetic.

1) **Visual** – Learn by seeing. (This can be accomplished through effective use of non-verbal communication and powerful graphics using PowerPoint, etc.)

2) **Auditory** – Learn by hearing. (This is where vocal variety is essential!)

3) **Kinesthetic** – Learn by doing (I always ask audience members to do something physically as a way to demonstrate what I am teaching – usually involves gesturing while presenting.)

Individual Prisms of Learning – Whenever possible, I try to learn as much as I can about the makeup of the audience well before my presentation. Not just demographic information, but information that may give me a clue as to individual experiences, such as job titles, educational background, place of birth, etc.

On presentation day, I'll usually ask the organizer to circulate an extremely brief two-question questionnaire to the participants (who can choose to remain anonymous):

1) What is the one thing you are most interested in learning at this presentation?

2) What is your most memorable communication experience and why?

The answers to these questions provide me with great insight. Also, depending on the size of the audience, I'll often start a presentation by asking individuals very basic, non-threatening questions such as:

1) Where are you from?

2) What is one thing that you want to hear me discuss?

3) What is the one trait you see in speakers that bothers you?

I ask these sorts of question in order to:

a) get more information about my audience;

b) get the audience directly involved;

c) turn the presentation into a conversation;

d) relax myself;

e) make sure I'm going to address what people want to hear.

It is about the audience – not me, after all!

Re-Engaging Your Audience

Let's say your presentation or lecture opened really well. Your message was well prepared, well delivered, and well supported. Your audience was engaged, the non-verbal feedback you received was energizing, and there was a lot of learning going on.

But, now you have reached the 10-minute mark of your presentation and you are starting to see some yawns. Heads are starting to be supported by fists. Eyes are glazing over. Posture goes from straight up and alert to slumping. Oh no!

You still have a number of points to hit! And, the information coming up is even more interesting. Why are they fading? How do you get them back?

First, it's important to understand that you may never know why they are fading. More important is knowing – how can you get your audience back? How do you keep the level of interest going?

While never a guarantee, here are a few strategies you can use to re-engage your audience:

1) **Ask questions** – The old failsafe. These questions should not be confrontational, probing, or personal. Basic questions that no one would find threatening will help to re-engage some of the audience members.

2) **Movement** – Step into the crowd. Leave the lectern behind. Step off the podium. The closer you get to your audience, the more re-engaged some of the audience members become.

3) **Demonstrate** – Demonstrating a concept while literally in the audience can be a powerful technique to re-engage people quickly. You can also ask for a volunteer from the audience to help demonstrate something.

4) **Self-Deprecating Humor** – If you "lightly" make fun of yourself and make the audience laugh, you will certainly get their attention. Some people advise against this because you don't want to raise questions about your confidence or credibility. However, if you make fun of yourself and it's something unrelated to the subject of expertise, you can get a few chuckles and re-engage the audience.

5) **Physical** – Get the audience to do something, anything. Move over one chair, stand up, or close their eyes. It just has to be non-confrontational, relevant to your topic, not too intimidating, and not singling out any one individual. Movement raises the energy level. Have them pick up a pen and write something down. Or draw something.

There are many ways to re-engage or re-energize an audience, but when you are in a tight situation, these techniques are quite effective.

Body Language – The "7 percent, 38 percent, 55 percent rule."

Over 40 years ago, Dr. Albert Mehrabian, a Professor from UCLA, released a study that, among other findings, concluded that when determining the meaning of a message, 55% of understanding was based on body (or facial) language, 38% based on tone of voice, and only 7% based on the words used.

That apparently means that 93% of communication is non-verbal. 93%!

Very powerful, and cited *ad nauseam* as "proof" that "what you say" is much less important than "how you say it."

All well and good except for the fact that the statistics are taken out of context. Way out of context. But don't take my word for it.

Professor Mehrabian was studying a very specific communication experience. Here is what he writes about his own study:

> "Total Liking = 7% Verbal Liking + 38% Vocal Liking + 55% Facial Liking.

> "Please note that this and other equations regarding relative importance of verbal and nonverbal messages were derived from experiments dealing with communications of feelings and attitudes (i.e., like-dislike). Unless a communicator is talking about their feelings or attitudes, these equations are not applicable. Also see references 286 and 305 in Silent Messages – these are the original sources of my findings."

While we have no idea just how significant non-verbal communication is by percentage, what is not debatable is that non-verbal communication plays a major role in any public presentation.

How you hold your hands, your posture, your eye contact, how you gesture, move or utilize facial expressions all influence how the audience receive, process and interpret the message, both positively and negatively.

There are countless body language "experts". The majority of advice from these "experts" is fairly rote – hold your hands this way, lack of eye contact means someone is lying, crossing your arms means you are defensive, pointing appears to be rude, and the list goes on and on. Some of this advice may be true. The operative word here is *may*.

Crossing your arms may mean you are in a defensive position, pointing may appear rude, and looking away may mean you are lying. Of course, crossed arms might be due to temperature, pointing may be inspirational to a certain audience, and lack of eye contact may be due to shyness, or a cultural bias.

The rationale: Every person is an individual, and what works for one person may, or may not, work for another.

I am an ardent believer that just as no two individuals are alike, no two speaking styles are alike; one body language principle may work for 95% of the population, but it may not work for you!

For example, steepled hands, made famous by a number of well-known public figures (President Clinton) can give an impression of arrogance to the audience; at the same time they may give an impression of thoughtfulness and reflection – if holding hands in the steepled position is a natural fit for the speaker.

While two different speakers will have two different styles, there are body language factors to be aware of. To communicate your message effectively, the one thing you want to do is prevent as many distractions to your audience as possible.

As stated in Forbes: "Every person has physical habits – in poker, you might call them 'tells,' – many of them are fidgets, for some people they're grooming gestures or postural things like a slouch." In everyday life these habits are no big deal, he says. But in an interview setting (or any other high stakes presentation setting) they can become a distraction, taking the focus away from your talents and onto your... bad hair day. "You're in a high-stakes situation with a stranger," he says. "There's a lot of pressure and an imbalanced power structure." If there's ever a time to get distracting (or worse, offensive) habits under control, this is it.

So what are some general "rules" to follow, potential pit-falls to watch out for, and basic strategies to think about to ensure that you are communicating as effectively as you can from a non-verbal perspective? In this section, we are going to focus on five non-verbal factors – Posture, Gestures, Arm/Hand Movements, Facial Expressions, and "Distractors."

1) **Posture**

Aim for a neutral spine. Posture should be the classic "sit up" or "stand up" straight, as if a string were tied from the top of your head to the ceiling. Do you want to experience what poor posture feels like? Tilt your hips forward, round your shoulders, and walk for five seconds. Then try it with your shoulders back, head straight, spine straight – the difference will be obvious. One trick – pinch your shoulder blades together with a cola can between them – this will open your chest dramatically. From that point, ease into a neutral spine, so that your shoulders are squared, rather than rounded.

Do you still need more evidence that an open posture will help you be a more effective presenter? Researchers at Harvard University found that engaging in powerful stances *before* presenting, when the audience could not even see the presenter, led to speakers being more confident, and actually increased temporary testosterone levels 20% and temporarily decreased the stress hormone cortisol.

2) Gestures

What do I do with my hands? This is easily one of the most frequent questions asked by almost every audience. My answer – what do you usually do with your hands? Use them!

Researchers have found that gesturing matters. Gesturing helps us remember, both as presenters and as audience members. Gesturing is intuitive, as most of us gesture all day without even realizing it.

In everyday interactions, we use our arms and hands when we talk, to varying degrees. I see this every day within my practice. I will tape an executive who will stand stiff as can be when presenting. I will then tape that same executive interacting in conversation with me. The difference – in conversation, the executive is significantly more animated. So how do we merge the two? How can your gesturing when presenting be more reflective of your gesturing while in everyday conversation?

3) Arm/Hand Movement

When it comes to gesturing and hand/arm movements, holding your hands a certain way is not the goal. The goal is to allow your hands and arms to be relaxed when you begin, and are most anxious, so that they can move freely as your comfort level increases.

Beginning with your arms at your sides, so that your arms and hands are free to move as you warm into your presentation, will help you to relax. If that is uncomfortable, a position, such as a steeple, that allows you to move your arms and hands freely will work as well.

As with everything, it depends on what makes you most comfortable. One thing to watch for – avoid distracting an audience!

Fast, repeated, or aggressive hand gestures should be kept to a minimum.

4) Facial Expressions

I can say with certainty that the non-verbal communications I find to be the most powerful in a presentation setting are facial expressions. Dr. Paul Ekman, psychology professor at University of California, San Francisco and expert on "micro-expressions" (and inventor of the term) has catalogued over 10,000 expressions we can make with the 43 facial muscles we have. 10,000!

When it comes to facial expressions, there are two rules to remember. First and foremost – be authentic. Dr. Ekman has proven we are far poorer at faking expressions than we think we are. Do you think that phony smile fooled the audience? Doubt it.

Second, allow people to see your expressions, and be in tune with your content so that your expressions match your content. Practicing expressions doesn't work. Being in the moment with the audience and your content, regardless of how nervous you are, does work. You will be more expressive than you think.

Practice will allow you to feel the emotion of what you are talking about, so that your expressions match your material. When you are happy, or talking about something that is happy in nature, you will smile.

Again, focus on making eye contact with your audience, and not just with one individual. If you are using notes, or a text, or a PowerPoint slide deck, do not speak while you are looking down, or to the side. Speak when you are looking at your audience – when you are looking down, try to remain silent.

5) "Distractors" - Grooming Gestures

"Grooming gestures" are common in high-pressure settings. It's just nervous energy and a natural desire to appear your best, and often they're not even an issue. Grooming gestures – playing with one's hair, fingernails, and jewelry – only become a problem when they distract the audience.

These nervous habits, which seem so intrinsic and unavoidable, are, in fact, the easiest to kick – at least for a limited time window such as a presentation.

I tend to roll my watch on my wrist, which is why it is not on my wrist when I present!

If you have long hair, pull it back or put it up so you don't flick it behind your ear repeatedly. I always tell people to avoid rings, watches, and jewelry on presentation day – if it's not there, you won't play with it. If you don't play with it, there's no chance of distracting your audience, which will keep their attention where it should be: focused on your presentation.

CHAPTER 4

PUBLIC SPEAKING 101

CHAPTER 4

PUBLIC SPEAKING 101

I) The Three Ps of a Polished Presenter

A polished presenter should:

1) Pause (Count: "1 Mississippi, 2 Mississippi," then begin.)
2) Prepare (Prior to presenting.)
3) Practice (A lot!)

II) Four Solutions for Better Presentations for Ages 16–60+

Solution # 1 – Slow Down!

No matter how knowledgeable, informed, or charismatic you are, you can still lose your audience's attention during a presentation.

How?

By not giving them enough time to process what you are saying.

So remind yourself that you are speaking to a group of people – you are not in a race. And:

> Slow Down!
> Slow Down!
> Slow Down!

Think fast. Talk slowly!

People want to hear what you have to say, but you also have to give them time to digest what you are saying. We all know that when you are addressing an audience, every second of silence feels like an eternity – to you! But how does it feel to your audience? It feels like – well, *a second of silence!*

So do whatever you need to do in order to take that *second* and slow yourself down. Take a brief pause, a breath, a sip of water, etc. Your audience will appreciate it.

Solution # 2 – Smile!

Did you know that smiling is contagious?

It will improve your confidence, the disposition of your audience, and will dramatically improve your speaking. Nothing will get the audience on your side faster than an authentic, genuine smile.

But what if you don't feel like smiling?

Let's say that you didn't exactly have a great morning. Perhaps, you had a fight with your significant other, your car wouldn't start, the bus never came, or you feel a cold coming on... so you may not be in a smiling mood.

Whatever you do, never ever fake it! You will not fool anyone and nothing spells insincerity like a fake, contrived smile.

However, there is ALWAYS something that can put a smile on your face. You are the only person who knows what that is. So the next time you find you need to access a genuine smile, try:

- Thinking about your kids, spouse, parent, best friend, or pet;
- Thinking about a funny situation or memory;
- Thinking about a favorite vacation spot.

Solution # 3 – Simple language

Leave the jargon, acronyms, and seven-syllable words at home. If someone does not understand what you are saying, your message will fail to resonate every time.

Solution # 4 – Succinct

All too often, an individual gives a terrific 45-minute presentation, but it falls flat.

Why?

It took 45 minutes to deliver it.

Stay brief. Less is more... always!

III) Seven Reminders Prior to Presenting

- Establish a presence immediately. Your presentation begins the moment someone sees you.
- To avoid lack of fluency (this includes false starts, repeated syllables and fillers such as ahh, um, err, like, etc.), pause instead.
- Always remember – it is never about you, it is always about the audience.
- Keep language simple and familiar (don't talk above the audience).
- Statistics, facts, and details must be understandable to everyone in the audience.

- Be present and in the moment.
- Handouts should come after – ensure that your audience pays attention to the presenter, rather than the handout.

IV) Eight Body Language Reminders

Follow these eight tips on body language:

1) Pay attention to posture. Keep your shoulders back and stand up straight.

2) Eye contact is crucial! Look at people; don't gaze over them or look past them.

3) Own your words. Let your emotions reflect what you are saying.

4) Be yourself.

5) There isn't one way to hold your hands. Don't flail, but do what's natural for you.

6) Be aware of your "grooming gestures".

7) Be aware of facial gestures – i.e. smirking.

8) Make sure your weight is evenly distributed – watch for distracting movements such as rocking, swaying, or pacing.

V) Vocal Delivery Elements – Examples

- Volume (loudness as in sound).
- Pitch (the frequency of the sound of a speaker's voice, low – high).
- Rate (pace or speed of speech).
- Tone (the pitch of a word used to determine or distinguish its meaning).
- Rhythm (systematic arrangement of sounds).

- Enunciation (articulation or pronunciation of words).
- Inflection (alteration in pitch or tone of the voice).

Social Psychology, Persuasion, and Public Speaking

Arizona State University professor and best-selling author, Dr. Robert Cialdini, is widely recognized as the leading authority on the science of influence.

Influencing others isn't about luck or magic – it's about science. Cialdini explains that there are proven ways to help make you more successful as an influencer. He identifies the six key principles of influence as: reciprocity, commitment/consistency, social proof, likeability, authority, and scarcity. Each of these principles is applicable to presenting and can be utilized to make more effective and impactful presentations.

So how can we apply these six concepts to public speaking?

1) **Reciprocity**

   Reciprocity in public speaking can take many forms. But, the most basic form is also one of the most effective. When you give the audience what's in it for them (their interest), they respond with a favorable reaction. One way to achieve this is by answering two questions when preparing your message. What does my audience care about? And why should my audience care?

   Another effective way to utilize reciprocity is to give your audience a verbal takeaway that was unexpected – a free tip, a useful piece of information, etc. Especially if you are an expert in your field and your audience has limited access to your expertise, a free and valuable piece of information can go a long way.

2) **Commitment/Consistency**

   Getting people to commit during a presentation can be challenging. One way that I have found successful is to ask questions based around your audience's interests. How do we identify those interests?

Through active preparation and research prior to the presentation – this leads to a clearer understanding of what the audience is looking for. Commitment is often gained prior to the presentation even beginning.

3) Social Proof

There is a reason that every toothpaste and gum sold on the market seems to be endorsed by "9 out of 10 dentists." This same principle can also work through the effective use of statistics and/or endorsements in a presentation.

Another effective technique is to speak with audience members prior to presenting, and reference them in your presentation. ("When we spoke earlier, Judy and Jane said... ") Just make sure it's nothing too embarrassing!

4) Likability

Likability is not something that can be taught. That being said, you can still help sway an audience to be pre-disposed to like you.

Here are a few suggestions:

a) Be authentic (i.e. be yourself).

b) Make your presentation about what your audience needs rather than what you want.

c) Be open.

d) When appropriate, genuinely smile.

5) Authority

Authority when presenting is usually established either (a) prior to your presentation or (b) through effectively demonstrating your ability to take detailed information and make it accessible to your audience.

Authority is not established by droning on and on about one's credentials or delving so deep into a subject matter that you are the only one who understands it. Neither is authority achieved through reliance on acronyms, jargon, or the use of sesquipedalian.

See, I just did it on purpose!

Sesquipedalian means having many syllables – if you are the only person who can pronounce or define a word, you will fail to influence anyone.

6) **Scarcity**

When it comes to communication, I equate scarcity with brevity. Entice your audience to want more!

After most presentations, the audience is worn out. Stand outside any conference venue and you will constantly hear, "I couldn't wait for that to end." Very rarely do you hear "That was riveting, I could have listened for hours." Aim for the latter.

A second way to utilize scarcity is to offer enticing information – just long enough to get your audience interested – and then… pause. Pause longer than usual. This will create a "scarcity effect" for a crucial moment in a presentation. An advanced scarcity technique is to allow that tantalizing information to serve as a feeder for the question and answer period.

CHAPTER 5

FEAR OF PUBLIC SPEAKING

CHAPTER 5

FEAR OF PUBLIC SPEAKING

Fear of Public Speaking – 25 Strategies

A random Internet search for "cures for fear of public speaking" produces over two million results. That's a shame. No matter how many books, courses, DVDs, websites, or snake oil salesmen promise to "cure" you of your fear of public speaking – it is never that simple or that easy. *And that is ok.*

The reality is that every executive has a rush of adrenaline before presenting – the normal "fight or flight" response.

Nervous energy, properly channeled, can actually enhance a presentation. So how can you alleviate the anxiety and effectively channel some of the tension prior to your next presentation?

Use these 25 strategies to help you deliver a great speech or presentation:

1) **Prepare:** The more prepared you are and the better handle you have on the material you are presenting, the better it will go.

2) **Practice:** Once you have prepared, you MUST practice. Practice

early and practice often. Rumor has it that Sir Winston Churchill practiced one hour for every minute of speech content he was delivering. Thus a five minute presentation = five hours of practice. How long are you practicing?

3) **Check out the room:** In this case, familiarity breeds comfort. Surprises on the day of a presentation are not fun and can increase anxiety tenfold. Check out your environment ahead of time. Is there a podium that you will be standing behind? What technology will you be using and does it work?

4) **Read the room:** While it's not always an option, when you have the opportunity to meet a few audience members beforehand, take it! Arrive ten minutes early and introduce yourself to a few people. If you are presenting mid-day, arrive before a key break to meet a few folks.

5) **"Seed" the audience:** Ask friends, associates, or colleagues that you like to come to your presentation. Also, talk to the conference organizers when you arrive so you know a few people. If possible, locate where familiar faces are sitting before you take the stage. The purpose of this is to have friendly faces to focus on if the anxiety starts to build.

6) **Remember the audience is on your side:** nine times out of ten, the audience is rooting for you to succeed – not wanting you to fail or fall flat. The audience is there to hear what you have to say. Assume they are excited about your speech or presentation.

7) **Breathing:** My three favorite breathing techniques – Three Deep Belly Breaths, Ujjayi Breathing, and the Alternate Nostril technique (these techniques are explained in further detail in tips 22 to 24 below).

8) **Listen to music:** If you were to watch a live boxing match, MMA competition, or NFL pre-game show, you'd see world-class athletes in the locker room listening to music. Listening to music helps athletes get in the zone, eliminate distractions, chase away

anxiety or negative thoughts, and get pumped up and excited. This technique also works really well prior to public speaking. So if you don't already have an iPod, you might want to get one. Listening to music beforehand can be a presenter's best friend.

9) **Visualization:** It works! Professional athletes, musicians, actors, and other highly successful people use the power of visualization techniques regularly. Professional boxers, when shadow boxing, do not throw random punches – they are visualizing an opponent and quite literally sparring with that visualization. Ballplayers do the same thing before approaching the plate. Use visualization to rehearse your speech in your mind. Not only see yourself delivering the speech, but visualize the audience reacting with excitement and interest.

10) **Body Movement:** A few minutes before taking the stage – "waggle" your jaw (lateral movement); bend forward and dangle your arms and let them shake; shake your hands over your head; and utilize simple stretches and isometric stretches. All of these movements, when incorporated with proper breathing, can warm the body, relax the mind, and calm your nerves.

11) **Body Movement, Part II:** As a former amateur boxer, nothing personally prepares me more for public speaking than light shadow boxing a few minutes before. I know a CEO who (literally) does 20 pushups prior to every earning's call. Focused movement helps even more than generic movement because it tends to take your thought process in a different direction.

12) **Do Sit-Ups:** There is a school of thought that suggests that constricting the abdominal wall prevents the production of epinephrine (a hormone associated with the fight or flight response). The most effective way to utilize this approach prior to speaking is to "crunch" and release the abdominal muscles while standing (lying down and doing sit-ups is probably not optimal!).

13) **Put the Pressure Elsewhere:** The more interactive your presen-

tation, the less pressure you will feel as the presentation becomes a true conversation. Most people are much more comfortable in a conversation than in delivering a formal presentation.

14) **Caffeine Free:** I always avoid copious amounts of caffeine (due to the epinephrine effect) as well as salty foods (to avoid drying out my mouth) on presentation day. I also tend to eat lighter, as this keeps me feeling sharp and light.

15) **Utilize Props:** A properly placed water bottle and well-timed break in the presentation to take a sip, not only gives the presenter a break for a few seconds, but can also be an effective technique to "reset" the audience.

16) **Work on your Open:** The first minute of the presentation is usually when your tension will peak. Having a well prepared, effective, and engaging opening will lessen the anxiety dramatically.

17) **The Restroom:** Don't laugh – on presentation day, the restroom is your ally. 10 or 15 minutes before presenting, head to the restroom to allow yourself the opportunity to breathe, listen to inspirational music, close your eyes, get into your zone, and of course use the bathroom. If called upon to do a last minute presentation, you will always be able to steal five minutes in the restroom – use it to pull yourself together and relax.

18) **Anxiety… Interrupted:** When you are less than five minutes from taking the stage, the anxiety is starting to build, your heart is pounding, and you keep telling yourself to calm down. One of my favorite techniques is to pick a random number over 1,000 and start counting backwards. Another technique is to count by multiples such as 7s, 9s, 11s, etc. It is not easy and allows for thought interruption – essentially halting the building anxiety.

19) **Anxiety… Distracted:** Maybe you are not a math wizard or the number technique is not effective for you; try instead to recite the alphabet backwards (mentally). Again, more thought pro-

cess disruption.

20) **Remember the Reality:** In working with thousands of speakers over the years, I have come to the realization that you are always more nervous than you actually appear. That's a good thing!

21) **Remember the Reality, Part II:** In most cases, your presentation is infinitely more important to you than to your audience members. The reality is that 99.9999…% of the time, the nightmare scenarios you envision will not come true.

22) **Breathing Exercise # 1:** Try three deep belly breaths (sounds like what it is). Slowly inhale through the nose for a count of 5–15 (15 is optimal). Meanwhile, keep one hand on your diaphragm and feel it enlarge as you inhale. Hold for 5–10 seconds and then exhale through your mouth slowly; again for a count of 5–15 seconds (15 is optimal). Repeat three times. This breathing technique is a great exercise to do a few minutes before you are going to speak.

23) **Breathing Exercise #2:** Ujjayi Breathing – also known as Oceanic or Victorious Breathing. This technique is remarkable. It is a yogic breathing technique that I first learned while struggling through Vinyasa yoga classes. It is similar to deep belly breathing; however, this time the mouth stays closed throughout the exercise.

24) **Breathing Exercise #3:** Alternate Nostril Breathing Technique (my favorite). All you need for this is your thumb, your pinkie finger, and your nose. To begin, simply cover your left nostril with your left thumb, and slowly and deeply inhale for 5 seconds to start (10 is optimal).

Then immediately cover your right nostril with your left pinkie finger, while keeping your left nostril pressed closed – at all times your mouth is closed as well, so at this point you are essentially holding your breath.

Again, hold for 5 seconds (10 is optimal). Then remove your left thumb from your left nostril and slowly exhale for a 10-second count. Wait 2 seconds and repeat the same technique, inhaling through your left nostril as your right nostril is still closed.

25) **Use Notes:** Memorization + anxiety = poor performance. Take the anxiety of memorization away by using an index card with key bullet points to help you stay on track. This removes the pressure of remembering what to say and the order in which you want to say it. Without worrying about memorization, your mind can stay clear and in the moment.

BONUS: There is one last technique that I frequently suggest to people who've had a traumatic public speaking experience in the past – that technique is scaling. After a traumatic experience, your memory tends to exaggerate how poorly the event went. The more time that goes by without that thought pattern being interrupted, the "bigger" the event feels. In this case, the more anxious you will feel prior to your next presentation. It's critical to break this pattern. This is done through scaling – finding low stakes …

So the next time you are about to present, do yourself a favor and take a deep breath and picture Sir Winston Churchill or Abraham Lincoln. Two of the greatest orators ever, both suffered from a fear of public speaking. Also, think about major Hollywood actors and actresses, many of whom also suffer from glossophobia (the fear of public speaking).

You are not alone! I can promise you that if you incorporate much of what you just read – your next presentation will be significantly better.

Fear of Public Speaking: Reframing "Fear"

"The only thing we have to fear is... fear itself."

—President Franklin D. Roosevelt

Most individuals experience some degree of anxiety and/or nervousness prior to presenting.

Every presenter has a rush of adrenaline prior to presenting. Having worked with thousands of speakers, I can attest to this. This angst seems to be independent of position or social standing – it doesn't matter if it is a CEO or a college student. Geography doesn't appear to be much of a factor either – whether the speaker is located in the Americas or Zimbabwe, the anxiety seems to follow. Nervous energy affects all of us.

This is a good thing.

That's right, it is a good thing.

Contrary to popular wisdom, "nervous" energy, properly channeled, and the physiological responses that follow will make for a more impactful presenter, and presentation.

One of the keys to channeling this "nervous energy" successfully is to understand what is actually happening when our acute stress response, or "fight or flight" response, kicks in.

Dr. Jeremy Jamieson, an expert on social stress and a Professor of Psychology at the University of Rochester, has studied extensively how stress impacts individuals in relation to risk, decision-making, and performance.

In a study conducted last year, Dr. Jamieson was able to determine that when an individual actually understands the physiological and psychological processes that occur when stress begins, and why these processes are actually very positive signs, he or she becomes much more adept at managing anxiety successfully.

"The problem is that we think all stress is bad," explains Jeremy Jamieson, the lead author on the study and an assistant professor of psychology at the University of Rochester. "We see headlines about 'Killer Stress' and talk about being 'stressed out.'" Before speaking in public, people often interpret stress sensations, like butterflies in the stomach, as a warning that something bad is about to happen, he says.

"But those feelings just mean that our body is preparing to address a demanding situation," explains Jamieson. "The body is marshaling resources, pumping more blood to our major muscle groups and delivering more oxygen to our brains. Our body's reaction to social stress is the same flight or fight response we produce when confronting physical danger. These physiological responses help us perform, whether we're facing a bear in the forest or a critical audience."

I have been working with Dr. Jamieson for the past few months, and have put his research and his materials into use with corporate clients when discussing ways to manage anxiety. The results when dealing with executives and professionals have been the same as Dr. Jamieson's results working with students. Simply understanding exactly what is happening to a person and the body's natural response when stress is initiated, why this is positive and how individuals in other fields utilize this advantageously has a positive effect on how individuals view and address anxiety prior to presenting.

Individuals tend to look no longer to eliminate the anxiety, but are more interested in learning how to manage it and "plateau" it – keep it from becoming all consuming. It also appears that individuals who performed earlier in life, whether former athletes, actors/actresses, musicians, etc., all tended to respond extremely well to the reframed understanding of the stress response.

Dr. Jamieson and I are partnering to conduct research to see how reframing can benefit as many individuals as possible. Reframing is not a new concept, but reframing the stress response through psychological and biological response as it relates to public speaking is new, exciting, and extremely powerful.

The graphic on the next page clearly illustrates exactly what is occurring, physiologically, as the acute stress response sets in.

Acute Stress Response - Public Speaking

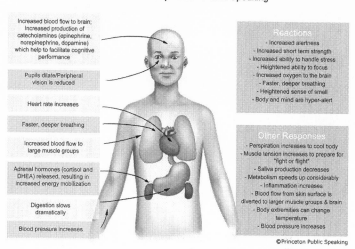

Increased blood flow to brain; Increased production of catecholamines (epinephrine, norepinephrine, dopamine) which help to facilitate cognitive performance

Pupils dilate/Peripheral vision is reduced

Heart rate increases

Faster, deeper breathing

Increased blood flow to large muscle groups

Adrenal hormones (cortisol and DHEA) released, resulting in increased energy mobilization

Digestion slows dramatically

Blood pressure increases

Reactions
- Increased alertness
- Increased short term strength
- Increased ability to handle stress
- Heightened ability to focus
- Increased oxygen to the brain
- Faster, deeper breathing
- Heightened sense of smell
- Body and mind are hyper-alert

Other Responses
- Perspiration increases to cool body
- Muscle tension increases to prepare for "fight or flight"
- Saliva production decreases
- Metabolism speeds up considerably
- Inflammation increases
- Blood flow from skin surface is diverted to larger muscle groups & brain
- Body extremities can change temperature
- Blood pressure increases

©Princeton Public Speaking

No One Can See You Sweat

"I know they are watching me tremble and sweat!"

"Can they see me shake?"

"I get so blotchy when I am nervous and I know that the audience can tell!"

I hear these questions and statements on a regular basis. Fear and anxiety before speaking publicly is nearly universal – it targets all of us, at different times and to varying degrees.

This includes me.

A common, recurring misconception is that the audience can perceive just how anxious, and just how nervous, you are. You may also feel that they are judging you. Your physiological responses to stress are apparent to everyone. The audience is focused on your anxiety.

This is simply untrue. And very detrimental, as the result is always the same – an increased stress response.

I have worked with thousands of speakers over the years and know that you are always more nervous than you appear. I have been telling speakers this for over a decade.

Having prepared speakers and witnessed presentations on five continents, I know this is one principle that is also universal. No matter the culture, region, context or audience. You may appear nervous, and the audience may see bits of sweat, but you *never* appear to be as nervous as you are feeling. The audience is simply not clued into your emotional state.

A study by Dr. Kenneth Savitsky and Dr. Thomas Gilovich*, from Cornell University Department of Psychology, confirms this.

The "illusion of transparency" typically refers to the "illusion" that a person's emotional and mental state is as obvious to others as it is to that individual. Hence, the *illusion* of transparency – you are typically not quite as "open of a book" as you may think.

Dr. Savitsky and Dr. Gilovich studied how the illusion of transparency affects speech anxiety. The studies confirmed that, in the authors' words:

> "..When individuals are called to speak in public, they do not appear as nervous as they think they do."

In addition, the second part of the study by Savitsky and Gilovich found that:

> "...Public speakers are often nervous over the (largely illusory) prospect that their nervousness is apparent to their audience—a concern that serves, ironically, to increase their nervousness."

Finally:

> "Speakers who were informed that their nervousness was not as apparent as they thought (but not participants who were merely reassured by the experimenter) were able to escape this spiral of nervousness and concern over leakage. As a result, they delivered speeches that were rated more positively than the speeches of those not so informed."

"Our results thus lend credence to the notion that 'the truth can set you free': Knowing the truth about the illusion of transparency set participants free from the cycle of anxiety that can plague those who engage in public speaking—and helped them deliver better speeches."[*]

In the 1980s, an advertising campaign for Dry Idea, an antiperspirant, told millions of people to, "Never let them see you sweat."

When it comes to public speaking, don't worry – they won't see you sweat.

---

*K. Savitsky and T. Gilovich "The Illusion of Transparency and the Alleviation of Speech Anxiety," *Journal of Experimental Social Psychology* 39 (2003): 618–625.

CHAPTER 6

MODERN ORATORY

CHAPTER 6

MODERN ORATORY

Demosthenes and Modern Oratory

Demosthenes is one of my favorite orators to study. Unfortunately, I never had the opportunity to see or hear him in person as he passed away in 322 BC. He was a prominent Greek statesman and legendary orator of ancient Athens, and some of his most famous (and my favorite) addresses were related to his opposition to King Phillip II of Macedon. Demosthenes is relevant to this book because of his dedication to practice and preparation.

Demosthenes actually grew up with a speech impediment. However, it didn't stop him from

Demosthenes (Wikipedia)

achieving his dream of becoming a great orator. As a child, he was ridiculed early and often for his deficiencies, but he never quit. Here are a few things he was rumored to have done to overcome his speech impediment and attain his goal:

- Self-corrected his defective elocution by practicing speaking with pebbles in his mouth;

- Prepared himself to overcome the distraction of noise by speaking in stormy weather on the seashore;

- Recited verses while running to improve his breathing and cadence;

- Sometimes passed two or three months in an underground cave practicing his oratory;

- While cave dwelling he would shave half of his head to prevent himself from leaving as a commitment to practicing.

While I would never encourage you to live in a cave or shave half your head, there are steps that everyone can take to practice and improve their speaking. Here are a few:

1) **Write it out** – I always write out every speech that I deliver. I then edit it and re-write it. I do this four or five times until I feel confident. It is at this point that I begin the process of shortening the speech to bullet points and then shortening the bullet points even more until there is nothing left to eliminate. Eventually, all that is left are key words and key phrases. This process not only helps to sharpen the presentation, it also helps to internalize it – after all, every re-write is a form of practice.

2) **Video tape yourself** – I have a studio that I use, although before I had a studio I used my garage. You can tape your speech anywhere that is private and quiet. Set up a video camera (almost all of which come with a remote) that adjusts the settings, and begin. This is an extremely effective way to get a feel not only for messaging and verbal delivery, but also for para-language, expressions, gestures, etc.

3) **Practice in front of people** – My wife is my biggest fan and sharpest critic. For the past nine years, I have practiced every speech or presentation in front of her multiple times. She always gives me very astute commentary. This works with co-workers, siblings, and anyone else whom you trust and whose opinion you respect as a listener.

4) **Audio tape yourself** – I often complement the use of a video camera with the use of a dictaphone so that I can focus entirely on my verbal delivery. A dictaphone is a small cassette recorder used to record speech for transcription at a later time.

5) **Exercise and deliver** – This technique is one that I "borrowed" from Demosthenes. I'll often run a few 100-yard sprints and then immediately retreat to my studio to practice and get my breathing right. You do not have to run sprints; any exercise that gets your heart rate up and adrenaline pumping can subtly mimic what your body feels like when beginning an address.

Demosthenes is not the only great orator who began life with a disadvantage.

Woodrow Wilson is not often one of the first figures that come to mind when remembering legendary orators of the past. He should be. The dedication and attention he gave to developing his communication skills from an early age may not make it into many public speaking books, but they should.

The challenges that the young Woodrow Wilson had to face as a communicator were significant. He was not a "natural." He was dyslexic, had attention issues, and did not exude confidence. But he studied the great orators. He practiced and practiced and practiced. He took advantage of every opportunity. This self-education paid off.

President Wilson made becoming a powerful, persuasive, effective communicator one of his top priorities as a student at Princeton University and as a young professor. This skill set served Wilson well as he went on to become President of Princeton University, Governor of New Jersey, and ultimately the President of the United States.

President Wilson has left us with many powerful orations. His diction, inflection, volume, and rate are notable in the only audio that I believe exists of Wilson speaking – a campaign address from 1912.

President Wilson's contributions to Princeton, New Jersey, and the United States are many. So are his contributions to oratory and public speaking. None are more important than the necessity of practice and preparation.

Steve Jobs – Public Speaking, Preparation, and Practice

Steve Jobs (Wikipedia)

The speed at which information travels has rendered most news dated within hours, days if a story really has "legs." To last through multiple news cycles is quite rare. However, the passing of Steve Jobs did just that, and for good reason. Over the past decade, very few (if any) executives have had the impact on how we communicate in the way that Steve Jobs did.

What made Steve Jobs so popular was not just about innovation or new technology. He was also an effective communicator. His public speaking skills had everything to do with fundamentals. An example being one that is crucial yet often ignored – extensive preparation. The preparation and practice that went into each product launch or public presentation was evident. Each presentation became an event in and of itself.

Two of my favorite Steve Jobs presentations:

1) *The launch of the original iPhone:*

Some key takeaways:

a) Very limited use of slides (no "Death by PowerPoint");

b) Limited content on each slide;

c) Effective use of movement;

d) Use of the "Power Pause;"

e) Effective gesturing;

f) Simple, conversational language. I am convinced that one of the reasons why Apple is the market leader is not only because of the ease-of-use of the product line, but also the ease-of-explanation as to how the products work and what they offer.

2) *Stanford Commencement – 2005*

This is one of the most moving speeches I have heard and seen in the past decade, and it affects me every time I watch it.

The key takeaways:

a) The use of story (amazing storytelling);

b) The use of repetition;

c) Use of summation (every story is neatly summarized with a memorable takeaway).

Look at these unforgettable words:

> "Almost everything – all external expectations, all pride, all fear of embarrassment or failure —these things just fall away in the face of death, leaving only what is truly important. Remembering that you are going to die is the best way I know to avoid the

trap of thinking you have something to lose. You are already naked. There is no reason not to follow your heart."

—Steve Jobs

As Simple As ABC – What Leaders Can Learn From Masterful Orators of the Past

Millions of meetings and presentations occur every day. Each of these presentations is meant to drive "someone" to do "something." And what do the vast majority of these presentations have in common?

Unfortunately, it's that they usually fail to get anyone to do anything.

There are so many noble causes led by charismatic, effective leaders – yet it is difficult for many of these leaders to establish a clear message that resonates and connects with the audience. And this is not due to the content or quality of the cause, but because we are all subject to information overload.

Still, masterful orators have succeeded in every generation. One factor that has not changed over time is the ability of a master orator to captivate and move audiences, and to attain levels of success that many thought were unachievable at the time. And each of them mastered the ABCs of communication.

The ABCs: Action, Brevity, and Conviction

Long before you learned to read or write, you needed to master your ABC. Communication is no different. Before one can create an effective message or master the details of public speaking, body language, gesturing, etc., one must master the ABC of communicating and messaging.

Over the past decade the ease, access to, and speed at which information travels has become blinding. Today, we have access to more information than we could have imagined a short time ago – and perhaps more than a human being could ever want or need. We have entered an information-age in which today's front page story is literally "yesterday's news." So how do you make sure your voice is "heard"? What are the "secrets" of master orators?

There are countless numbers of books written on communication, public speaking, and presenting – many with very good advice and some semblance of practicality. These books are read, re-read, and widely discussed. However, what's missing from many of them? Not necessarily the "how" but more importantly the "what."

What do successful messages have in common? What do those who have delivered these messages have in common? They all follow the ABC of communication.

Put simply, Sir Winston Churchill did not use PowerPoint. Franklin Roosevelt did not put on slideshows. Abraham Lincoln did not have the media of television and radio available to disseminate his message to the masses. However, these leaders all mastered basic, fundamental communication principles, including the ABC.

A) Action (a call to)

Chances are that a leader wants to move an audience. He or she wants to motivate, persuade, or influence an audience to do something, i.e. take action. This idea of doing something can range from taking physical action (such as volunteering, protesting, advocating, demonstrating, or letter writing) to action that is less physically active (such as voting) to something that is not physical at all (such as changing a thought process, goal, desire, or in some instances the course of life itself).

President John F. Kennedy's Inaugural Address has been one of the two most frequently published addresses in the last 60 years. The most famous statement in the address is:

> "And so, my fellow Americans: ask not what your country can do for you – ask what you can do for your country. My fellow

citizens of the world: ask not what America will do for you, but what together we can do for the freedom of man."

It is remarkable how powerful these lines were, not only when they were originally delivered, but also now six decades later.

In fact, President Kennedy's daughter, Caroline Kennedy, sees this call-to-action as one of the greatest legacies of her father. When describing the inspiration for the John F. Kennedy Profile in Courage Award she notes:

> "Ever since I was a little girl, people have told me that my father changed their lives. They got involved in public service, in government, in their communities because he asked them to and they wanted to be part of something larger and better than themselves. President Kennedy's Inaugural challenge – 'Ask not what your country can do for you; ask what you can do for your country' – inspired a generation in the 1960s that transformed our nation with courage and dedication and in turn inspired those who followed. To me, that is one of his greatest legacies, and it is in them that his spirit lives on."
> — Caroline Kennedy, *TIME Magazine*, 2007.

Why was this speech so effective? Its effectiveness turns on the fact that it was a call-to-action.

What is rarely debated is its effectiveness in motivating individuals well after the speech was given. In fact, the Sixth Floor Museum at Dealey Plaza – the museum that chronicles the assassination and legacy of President Kennedy – hosts a special exhibit entitled "Call to Action."

B) Brevity/simplicity

There are quotes throughout history emphasizing the benefit of brevity when speaking or presenting in public. From Roman statesman, scholar, and orator, Cicero, who stated, "Brevity is the best recommendation in speech, whether in senator or orator" to President

Franklin D. Roosevelt, who said, "Be sincere; be brief; be seated," brevity while speaking has long been viewed as a virtue.

There is no better example of "brevity" than President Abraham Lincoln's Gettysburg Address. There have been countless books written about this famous address and Presidents throughout history have studied these words. The first six words of this address, "Four score and seven years ago" are ingrained in every elementary schoolchild's memory in America. Many facts surrounding the address have been debated. Two are not.

First, Abraham Lincoln was not the keynote speaker; Edward Everett, a sought after orator of the day, was. Edward Everett was considered one of the greatest orators of his time, and had been designated as the keynote speaker for the dedication of the Gettysburg monument. Second, Edward Everett's speech was over 15,000 words long and lasted over two hours, while Lincoln's Gettysburg Address was 246 words long and lasted between two and four minutes.

Edward Everett quickly recognized the virtue of brevity, commenting to President Lincoln, "Mr. Lincoln, if I could have come as near striking the keynote of this occasion in three hours as you did in three minutes, I should be better satisfied with my performance."

President Lincoln was able to deliver so much power in so few words because it was so brief.

Today, the Gettysburg Address is revered as one of the greatest speeches ever delivered. President Lincoln is often regarded as one of the greatest leaders in U.S. history, and Edward Everett's name is barely known. Why? While it is not possible to study the cadence, tone, delivery, etc. of a speech given nearly 165 years ago, one thing that can be studied is the speech itself.

President Lincoln was able to deliver so much power in so few words because it was so brief. There was no time for his message to get diluted, for his thoughts to twist and turn, and for his audience to lose their focus. The President was able to grab the attention of his audience immediately and hold onto it. No superfluous words, no unnecessary sentences, and no dilution of message. Brevity seized the day then and brevity will seize the day now.

C) Conviction (character)

"He wasn't a natural orator, not at all. His voice was raspy. A stammer and a lisp often marred many of his speeches. Nor was his appearance attractive... Short and fat, he was also stoop-shouldered."

– from *Churchill: A Study in Oratory*

Winston Churchill
(Library of Congress)

Add to that Sir Winston Churchill's quick sarcasm and strong opinions – characteristics that were certainly not universally liked or accepted – and you begin to wonder how Churchill was able to persuade and influence so effectively?

Churchill used his conviction to will not only his nation, but also the entire world to change course. The sheer will and conviction of Churchill, his words, and his beliefs, may have been as beneficial to the British cause as the logic of his argument, the credibility of the speaker, or his emotional appeal.

One can argue that the "We Shall Fight on the Beaches" speech was also a call-to-action, which it was. This speech can and has been studied and utilized to demonstrate how to give a speech, how to use repetition, and a host of other "how to" lessons. This speech offers something for everyone. What does it offer a leader today? It offers evidence of the power of conviction when speaking or presenting a message.

Listening to this speech, one can feel the raw power, feeling, emotion, and drive in Churchill's every word. Churchill had railed against the Nazi regime, often without an audience and long before it was in vogue to do so. When opinion turned, there was no questioning his conviction. It is hard to imagine a British citizen not being inspired upon hearing the final paragraph of this inspiring address:

> "We shall go on to the end, we shall fight in France, we shall fight on the seas and oceans, we shall fight with growing confidence and growing strength in the air, we shall defend our Island, whatever the cost may be, we shall fight on the beaches, we shall fight on the landing grounds, we shall fight in the fields and in the streets, we shall fight in the hills; we shall never surrender, and even if, which I do not for a moment believe, this Island or a large part of it were subjugated and starving, then our Empire beyond the seas, armed and guarded by the British Fleet, would carry on the struggle, until, in God's good time, the New World, with all its power and might, steps forth to the rescue and the liberation of the old."

His conviction never wavered, even when he was not in power. This was evident in his communication to the British Empire's citizens, her allies, and her enemies.

So what? What does this information mean to the leader of a company, whether it has 2 employees or 20,000? Or to a not-for-profit leader trying passionately to motivate or attract supporters? Or what is its significance to a political candidate running for a local or federal office?

Chances are, barring some unforeseen circumstance, the vast majority of leaders will never: (a) have to communicate to as large an audience as a President or Prime Minister does; (b) have the resources available that a world leader does; and (c) have the ability to reach the masses through paid or earned media the way a world leader does.

So how can a leader utilize the ABCs of communication effectively in light of the above?

A) Action

A speech or presentation given without a call-to-action is a speech or presentation not worth giving. I have come to the conclusion that if there is no desired action or re-action on the part of the speaker or presenter, there is very little reason to speak or present at all. The list of potential actions a speaker may desire is endless: support, opposition, motivation, dissuasion, encouragement, education, organization, etc.

In order to utilize this principle effectively, I believe the best course of action for a leader to take is to ask him or herself prior to developing a talk, presentation, speech, meeting outline, or press conference to answer the following three questions – as they are fundamental in both determining the message and its effectiveness:

1) What do I want to accomplish?

2) What is the desired result? What do I want the audience to do?

3) Who cares? Why should they care?

These questions, with proper introspection and preparation, will lead the leader in terms of developing a message with a clear call-to-action.

If there is no desired action or re-action on the part of the speaker or presenter, there is very little reason to speak or present at all.

B) Brevity

Once a basic message and call-to-action have been determined, the hard work of deciding exactly how to develop and deliver this message begins. Determining what words to use, what phrases to use, how much detail to give, and how much information to provide are the logical next steps. Once you have figured out what you are trying to accomplish, you need to figure out how to accomplish it. And, in communication, there is no substitute for brevity.

In the vast majority of presentations (speeches, debates, press conferences, announcements, etc.), the one universal similarity is the tendency to include more information than is necessary to convey the message. This frequently leads to message dilution and often to the message getting lost completely.

Look to advertisers, or more importantly, copywriters and newspaper editors, for excellent examples of how to use extreme brevity to attract attention – headlines. Newspaper and magazine headlines are created with one of two purposes in mind. Either (a) get the customer interested enough to purchase the publication, or if the publication has been purchased, (b) get the customer to read the article following the headline.

While never as brief as a headline, a leader should utilize brevity in order to whet the palate of the audience, communicate a core message, or get the audience interested in and desiring more information – all leading to the generation of action.

Leaders can use the cornerstone of brevity effectively by answering the three questions above, and then asking what information is absolutely necessary to elicit the desired action or reaction. The most effective way to do this is through preparation and practice, and the effective "whittling down" of content until the core message and crucial information is all that is left.

As famous French writer Antoine de Saint-Exupery (author of *The Little Prince*) said so eloquently, "Perfection is achieved, not when there is nothing more to add, but when there is nothing left to take away." Every leader should think about his or her communication in the same light.

C) Conviction

The perfect call-to-action, with the perfect amount of information, delivered in perfect fashion – will still fall flat if the audience does not believe that the speaker believes in what is being communicated. Of the three cornerstones, conviction is at its core both the simplest and the most difficult cornerstone to implement. And the simplicity and difficulty both stem from the same place – within the speaker.

It is the simplest because it is either there or it is not. It is the most difficult because it cannot be learned or faked. A leader either strongly believes in his or her message or he or she doesn't. One thing every leader should realize: an audience can sense how much conviction is behind a message.

So how can a leader effectively utilize conviction?

Put simply, make absolutely certain that you believe in what you are about to say prior to saying it. No amount of practice and preparation will help a leader convey conviction if he or she simply does not fully believe in what he or she is communicating.

And – ABC) Audience

Again, most leaders will not have the opportunity to reach the masses in the way that a President or Prime Minister can. But that makes the utilization of the ABCs even more critical.

While everything a President says and does is closely scrutinized, chances are if he or she has an "off day" or mis-speaks, he or she will have the opportunity to rebound and "message correct" in the future. The audience will still be there.

There is a strong possibility that if a regular speaker fails to connect and communicate a message effectively, even once, the chance to reach that same audience may not come again. This makes it crucial to invest the time to determine clearly what your message is, be able to capture and communicate that message as simply and briefly as possible, and make sure that prior to communicating this message you feel and believe the message you are about to deliver.

You may not be able to reach the number of people that the President can, but the opportunity exists for a leader to spread his or her message well beyond the limitations that existed before. The barriers to sharing information are being torn down all around us, making it possible to reach not only those you know already, but those that may have an interest in your cause or company continents away.

But there are so many voices out there clamoring to be heard – you may not get a second chance if you lose their attention. So you must master and follow the ABCs. They are the cornerstones and building blocks of all successful communication.

In an age where technology changes the ways in which we communicate each and every day, the alphabet still exists as the bedrock of the English language, the very foundation of our words, and the basics with which we formulate thoughts and opinions. The same holds true of the ABC of communication. No matter what the technology, medium, venue, audience, or audience size, there is simply no greater way to achieve communication success or convey a message effectively than by following your ABC.

CHAPTER 7

LESSONS FROM THE GREAT ORATORS

CHAPTER 7

LESSONS FROM THE GREAT ORATORS

Five Public Speaking Lessons from President Abraham Lincoln

"Four score and seven years ago our fathers brought forth on this continent, a new nation, conceived in Liberty, and dedicated to the proposition that all men are created equal.

Now we are engaged in a great civil war, testing whether that nation or any nation so conceived and so dedicated, can long endure. We are met on a great battlefield of that war. We have come to dedicate a portion of that field, as a final resting

Abraham Lincoln
(Library of Congress)

place for those who here gave their lives that that nation might live. It is altogether fitting and proper that we should do this.

But, in a larger sense, we cannot dedicate – we cannot consecrate – we cannot hallow – this ground. The brave men, living and dead, who struggled here, have consecrated it, far above our poor power to add or detract. The world will little note, nor long remember what we say here, but it can never forget what they did here. It is for us the living, rather, to be dedicated here to the unfinished work which they who fought here have thus far so nobly advanced. It is rather for us to be here dedicated to the great task remaining before us – that from these honored dead we take increased devotion to that cause for which they gave the last full measure of devotion – that we here highly resolve that these dead shall not have died in vain – that this nation, under God, shall have a new birth of freedom – and that government of the people, by the people, for the people, shall not perish from the earth."

—President Abraham Lincoln

There are some key public speaking and communication lessons that everyone – whether in a boardroom or on a blog – can gain from studying this remarkable address.

1) **Be brief** – While there is always debate surrounding the Gettysburg Address, this much we know – the entire address was under 300 words and took less than three minutes to deliver (maybe closer to two minutes). Think about that the next time you address the Board, your constituents, the jurors, or the venture capitalists from whom you are requesting $15 million.

2) **You are *always* the featured speaker** – The keynote speaker 147 years ago was Edward Everett, who spoke for nearly two hours; Lincoln was an afterthought. If you are introducing someone or closing an event, treat it as though you are the featured presenter.

3) **Simple word selection works** – Try to avoid 100-point Scrab-

ble words, fancy jargon, or acronyms. Lincoln's word choice was clear and effective – regardless of each listener's education level.

4) **Paint a picture when you speak** – While not always referenced as such, the Gettysburg Address is a story. Lincoln used his words to paint a picture of this story.

5) **Motivate** – The Gettysburg Address provides clear direction as to what Lincoln wanted listeners to do – show support for the (very) shaky governmental structure.

Does this mean that if a blog post is over 300 words or a speech takes over two to three minutes that it is ineffective? No. It means that when speaking or writing, focus on what the audience really wants and needs to know, rather than just on what you want to say. Brevity always wins.

Five Lessons from William Bourke Cochran

William Bourke Cochran, in my opinion, may be one of the greatest speakers of all time. Who is William Bourke Cochran, you ask? And, how can I make such a bold statement? After all, I never witnessed him speak, as he passed away well before speeches were recorded on video.

I have been fascinated by the ability of an individual to influence through spoken word since I was a young boy. I am often asked which orator has had the biggest impact on me, and my oratorical role model

Bourke Cochran
(Library of Congress)

is Sir Winston Churchill. And who was Churchill's oratorical role model? William Bourke Cochran.

William Bourke Cochran, a Congressman from New York City in the early 1900s, was described in his day as the greatest orator in the land. He also served as an oratorical role model for a young Winston Churchill. It was not just Churchill who held Cochran in such high regards as an orator – it was the vast majority of his peers.

The sad fact is that William Bourke Cochran might be the greatest speaker whom no one knows about today. Books on him are few and far between, with my favorite being *Becoming Winston Churchill: The Untold Story of Young Winston and his American Mentor*, written by Michael McMenamin and Curt Zoller. There are not many Internet resources dedicated to Cochran, and even his Wikipedia entry is lacking.

Cochran was noted for his ability to move colleagues and constituents to support causes or even change positions due to his magnificent oratory.

Churchill once wrote to Cochran about Cochran, saying, "…There are few more fascinating experiences than to watch a great mass of people under the wand of a magician…."

Congressman Charles O'Brien (D-NJ), said the following at Cochran's Memorial Service:

> "Much has been said and written about his ability as an orator. For ages to come, his will be the standard upon which men of similar genius will be judged. In all the history of the world, no man has surpassed and few have equaled him."

Finding information about Cochran might be difficult, but there are clear lessons that young Churchill and many other leaders took away from him. Here are a few:

1) **Rhythm** – Every speech should have a rhythm although most don't. Cochran was known for his rhythmic speeches.

2) **Presence** – Cochran knew the power of presence and used his body, gestures, and voice to captivate and move the audience. So can you – no matter your body type, height, weight, or voice. You can use your best qualities to your advantage. Everyone has natural strengths; it's just a matter of finding them.

3) **Conversational language** – Every presentation or speech is a conversation – both verbally and non-verbally. Use your language and body language to affect the audience.

4) **Power of Delivery** – It's not only what you say, but also how you say it. Deliver your speech with confidence! Did you know that people who speak well are perceived as more competent, trustworthy, and knowledgeable?

5) **Subject Matter Expertise** – Cochran was not only known for his oratorical skill, but also for his mastery of the subject upon which he was speaking. So be an expert or really understand what you are speaking about. It's much better to talk about a subject you understand than just to memorize a speech.

Seven Lessons from Dr. Martin Luther King, Jr.

On August 28, 1963, Dr. Martin Luther King, Jr. delivered his "I Have a Dream" speech from the steps of the Lincoln Memorial. This 17-minute address is an amazing oratorical display. Very few people will ever address an issue as important (with the whole world watching); however, everyone can learn valuable lessons about presenting from this speech. Here are a few:

Martin Luther King
(Library of Congress)

1) **Cadence** – King's control of cadence is simply amazing. No

words are lost, and key pauses exist throughout the entire address. One technique to try to learn cadence is to read great speeches along with the soundtrack of the person delivering it.

2) **Rhythm** – Great speeches have great cadence and great rhythm. This speech had both.

3) **Inflection** – During this speech, King used inflection to stress clearly different words. With the proper use of inflection, there should be no confusion in the audience as to which point you are trying to make.

4) **Eye Contact** – King read quite a bit of his speech, but when he reached crucial sections, he looked right at the 200,000 people watching him.

5) **Rhetorical Tools** – King's use of *anaphora* – repeating a sequence of words at the beginning of neighboring clauses, thereby lending them emphasis. For example, "I have a dream... I have a dream..."

6) **Passion** – Is there any question whether King felt every single word as he delivered it? While your presentation may not be on a subject as personal or important to you, there needs to be something that you feel strongly about around the subject matter – find it.

7) **Practice** – It is rumored that King went off-script at the end of this address. However, it is also rumored that he practiced the vast majority of this address extensively prior to delivering it. Chances are, you are probably not as orally gifted as King so if he had to practice, you should practice too.

Remember, a speech is poetry: cadence, rhythm, imagery, and passion!

"A speech reminds us that words, like children, have the power to make dance the dullest beanbag of a heart."

—Peggy Noonan

Seven Lessons from Nelson Mandela

"When a man has done what he considers to be his duty to his people and his country, he can rest in peace. I believe I have made that effort and that is, therefore, why I will sleep for the eternity."

—Nelson Mandela, 1994

Nelson Mandela
(Wikipedia)

Nelson Mandela's life, legacy, and contribution to humanity will be studied for generations to come.

Mandela's skill as a wordsmith and communicator will also be studied for generations to come.

Whether in his longer address at the opening of his trial 50 years ago in 1964, or in his statement upon his release from prison in 1990, Mandela clearly understood the power of words and language.

The sentences that Mandela closed with, both prior to imprisonment and upon his release, were carefully chosen, extremely powerful, and symbolize why he is one of the most revered figures in modern history. The final lines clearly articulate his message:

"During my lifetime I have dedicated myself to this struggle of the African people. I have fought against white domination, and I have fought against black domination. I have cherished the ideal of a democratic and free society in which all persons live together in harmony and with equal opportunities. It is an ideal which I hope to live for and to achieve. But if needs be, it is an ideal for which I am prepared to die."

April 24, 1964
February 11, 1990

Mandela is certainly one of the most effective orators in modern history. Mandela's contributions to oratory and public speaking are many. Here are seven:

1) **Message Development** – When reading or listening to a Mandela speech (unfortunately there are few videos available of Mandela pre-imprisonment) his message is well constructed, audience appropriate, and consistent.

2) **Expression** – Nelson Mandela was masterful at utilizing his facial muscles for emphasis whenever he spoke. His smile could light up any room, and served as a huge highlighter when delivering key lines. I am always particularly moved by his eyes – at some points when he speaks, even on a video clip, it often seems that he is looking directly at you. Which leads to...

3) **Presence** – Mandela carried himself like a man 20 years younger than his age. When speaking, it was clear he knew the power of nonverbal communication – he stood straight, shoulders back, no swaying, no rocking. He spoke with a measured cadence, and utilized pausing effectively to emphasize key points. Before he spoke, it was clear that a leader was on stage.

4) **Perfection** – One of the first lessons would-be orators can learn from Mandela is that no speaker is perfect. No speaker. Some of Mandela's speeches were quite long and occasionally he would read directly from a script for long stretches with little eye contact. And Mandela and his speeches are routinely included in lists and books citing great historical speakers and speeches.

5) **Rhetorical Devices** – Like legendary orators before him, Mandela artfully utilized rhetorical devices to support his messag-

ing. Examples of devices include metaphor, anaphora, allusion, and repetition.

6) **Quotations** – One of the greatest gifts that Mandela has left future orators is a treasure chest of powerful, impactful quotations to open or close a speech or presentation; or to utilize to support key messages. The Nelson Mandela Centre of Memory offers an entire book of his quotations – visit www.nelsonmandela.org for more information.

7) **Word Selection** – Nelson Mandela clearly understood the power of words and language. In a world where public figures often discount the power of word selection, Mandela clearly knew that many, many people were listening closely to every word he spoke. His address upon release from prison illustrates Mandela's respect for the power of word selection.

As he stated when closing the 13th Annual International Aids Conference in Durban in 2000:

> "It is never my custom to use words lightly. If twenty-seven years in prison have done anything to us, it was to use the silence of solitude to make us understand how precious words are and how real speech is in its impact on the way people live and die."

CHAPTER 8

SPEECH ANALYSIS

CHAPTER 8

SPEECH ANALYSIS

Rhetorical Devices — 10 Examples

Alliteration

The use of words beginning with or containing the same letter or sound.

"..the poison we must purge from our politics.."
—Senator Barack Obama

Anaphora

Repetition of words at the beginning of consecutive phrases.

"We shall go on to the end…"—Sir Winston Churchill

"I have a dream…"—Dr. Martin Luther King Jr.

"Let freedom ring…"—Dr. Martin Luther King Jr.

Anthimeria (verbing)

Taking a noun and turning it into a verb.

Googling
Tweeting
Amazoning
Texting

Anthropomorphism

Giving non-human beings human characteristics.

The camera loves you
The trees called to him
The wind screamed

Assonance

The rhyming of one word with another in the accented vowel.

"If I bleat when I speak, it's because I just got fleeced."
—Al Swearengen in *Deadwood*

Asyndeton

Consecutive words or phrases linked together WITHOUT conjunctions.

"We shall fight..."—Sir Winston Churchill

"Go back to Mississippi, go back to Alabama, go back to South Carolina, go back to Georgia..."
—Dr. Martin Luther King Jr.

Chiasmus

Corresponding pairs that do not follow the typical a-b; a-b; instead they follow a-b; b-a:

"It is not the end of the beginning; it is the beginning of the end. Freedom requires religion; religion requires freedom."
—Mitt Romney

(Basic) Contrasts

Beginning – End; Sharp – Dull; Win – Loss

> "Never was so much owed by so many to so few."
> —Sir Winston Churchill

Epistrophe

Repetition of words at the end of consecutive phrases.

> "...my friends ... my friends."—anything by John McCain
> "...Yes we can ... Yes we can."—President Barack Obama
> "...You'll see me ... You'll see me."—Ghost of Tom Joad

Hypophora

Asking a question (rhetorical) and immediately answering it

> "So what is a hypophora? A hypophora is a rhetorical device..."

Onomatopoeia

Words that resemble the sounds they make (VERY effective for speeches)

> *Splat*
> *Bang*

Polysndeton

Consecutive words or phrases linked together WITH conjunctions.

> "Send lawyers, guns and money."—Warren Zevon

Famous Speeches

Below you will find transcripts from two of the most powerful speeches in United States history. A few examples of the use of rhetorical devices have been identified for you. Many, many more exist in each speech. Try to uncover as many as possible.

Speech 1 - Dr. Martin Luther King Jr.

"I Have A Dream"

August 28, 1963

Five score years ago [allusion], a great American, in whose symbolic shadow we stand today, signed the Emancipation Proclamation. This momentous decree came as a great beacon light of hope to millions of Negro slaves who had been seared in the flames of withering injustice. It came as a joyous daybreak to end the long night of their captivity.

But one hundred years later [anaphora], the Negro still is not free. One hundred years later, the life of the Negro is still sadly crippled by the manacles of segregation and the chains of discrimination [metaphor]. One hundred years later, the Negro lives on a lonely island of poverty in the midst of a vast ocean of material prosperity. One hundred years later, the Negro is still languishing in the corners of American society and finds himself an exile in his own land.

So we have come here today to dramatize a shameful condition. In a sense we have come to our nation's capital to cash a check. When the architects of our republic wrote the magnificent words of the Constitution and the Declaration of Independence, they were signing a promissory note to which every American was to fall heir. This note was a promise that all men, yes, black men as well as white men, would be guaranteed the unalienable rights of life, liberty, and the pursuit of happiness.

It is obvious today that America has defaulted on this promissory note insofar as her citizens of color are concerned. Instead of honoring this sacred obligation, America has given the Negro people a bad check, a check which has come back marked "insufficient funds." But we refuse to believe that the bank of justice is bankrupt. We refuse to believe that there are insufficient funds in the great vaults of opportunity of this nation. So we have come to cash this check – a check that will give us upon demand the riches of freedom and the security of justice.

We have also come to this hallowed spot to remind America of the fierce urgency of now. This is no time to engage in the luxury of cooling off or to take the tranquilizing drug of gradualism. Now is the time to make real the promises of democracy. Now is the time to rise from the dark and desolate valley of segregation to the sunlit path of racial justice. Now is the time to lift our nation from the quick sands of racial injustice to the solid rock of brotherhood. Now is the time to make justice a reality for all of God's children.

It would be fatal for the nation to overlook the urgency of the moment. This sweltering summer of the Negro's legitimate discontent will not pass until there is an invigorating autumn of freedom and equality. Nineteen sixty-three is not an end, but a beginning. Those who hope that the Negro needed to blow off steam and will now be content will have a rude awakening if the nation returns to business as usual. There will be neither rest nor tranquility in America until the Negro is granted his citizenship rights. The whirlwinds of revolt will continue to shake the foundations of our nation until the bright day of justice emerges.

But there is something that I must say to my people who stand on the warm threshold which leads into the palace of justice. In the process of gaining our rightful place we must not be guilty of wrongful deeds. Let us not seek to satisfy our thirst for freedom by drinking from the cup of bitterness and hatred.

We must forever conduct our struggle on the high plane of dignity and discipline [assonance]. We must not allow our creative protest to degenerate into physical violence. Again and again we must rise to the majestic heights of meeting physical force with soul force. The marvelous new militancy which has engulfed the Negro community must not lead us to a distrust of all white people, for many of our white brothers, as evidenced by their presence here today, have come to realize that their destiny is tied up with our destiny. They have come to realize that their freedom is inextricably bound to our freedom. We cannot walk alone.

As we walk, we must make the pledge that we shall always march ahead. We cannot turn back. There are those who are asking the devotees of civil rights, "When will you be satisfied?" [hypophora] We can never be satisfied as long as the Negro is the victim of the unspeakable horrors of police brutality. We can never be satisfied, as long as our bodies, heavy with the fatigue of travel, cannot gain lodging in the motels of the highways and the hotels of the cities. We cannot be satisfied as long as the Negro's basic mobility is from a smaller ghetto to a larger one. We can never be satisfied as long as our children are stripped of their selfhood and robbed of their dignity by signs stating "For Whites Only". We cannot be satisfied as long as a Negro in Mississippi cannot vote and a Negro in New York believes he has nothing for which to vote. No, no, we are not satisfied, and we will not be satisfied until justice rolls down like waters and righteousness like a mighty stream [simile].

I am not unmindful that some of you have come here out of great trials and tribulations. Some of you have come fresh from narrow jail cells. Some of you have come from areas where your quest for freedom left you battered by the storms of persecution and staggered by the winds of police brutality.

You have been the veterans of creative suffering. Continue to work with the faith that unearned suffering is redemptive.

Go back to Mississippi, go back to Alabama, go back to South Carolina, go back to Georgia, Go back to Louisiana [asyndeton], go back to the slums and ghettos of our northern cities, knowing that somehow this situation can and will be changed. Let us not wallow in the valley of despair.

I say to you today, my friends, so even though we face the difficulties of today and tomorrow, I still have a dream. It is a dream deeply rooted in the American dream.

I have a dream [anaphora] that one day this nation will rise up and live out the true meaning of its creed: "We hold these truths to be self-evident: that all men are created equal."

I have a dream that one day on the red hills of Georgia the sons of former slaves and the sons of former slave owners will be able to sit down together at the table of brotherhood.

I have a dream that one day even the state of Mississippi, a state sweltering with the heat of injustice [metaphor] sweltering with the heat of oppression, will be transformed into an oasis of freedom and justice.

I have a dream that my four little children will one day live in a nation where they will not be judged by the color of their skin but by the content of their character [alliteration].

I have a dream today.

I have a dream that one day, down in Alabama, with its vicious racists, with its governor having his lips dripping with the words of interposition and nullification; one day right there in Alabama, little black boys and black girls will be able to join hands with little white boys and white girls as sisters and brothers.

I have a dream today.

I have a dream that one day every valley shall be exalted, every hill and mountain shall be made low, the rough places will be made plain, and the crooked places will be made straight, and the glory of the Lord shall be revealed, and all flesh shall see it together.

This is our hope. This is the faith that I go back to the South with. With this faith we will be able to hew out of the mountain of despair a stone of hope. With this faith we will be able to transform the jangling discords of our nation into a beautiful symphony of brotherhood. With this faith we will be able to work together, to pray together, to struggle together, to go to jail together, to stand up for freedom together, knowing that we will be free one day.

This will be the day when all of God's children will be able to sing with a new meaning, "My country, 'tis of thee, sweet land of liberty, of thee I sing. Land where my fathers died, land of the pilgrim's pride, from every mountainside, let freedom ring."

And if America is to be a great nation this must become true. So let freedom ring from the prodigious hilltops of New Hampshire. Let freedom ring from the mighty mountains of New York. Let freedom ring from the heightening Alleghenies of Pennsylvania!

Let freedom ring from the snowcapped Rockies of Colorado!

Let freedom ring from the curvaceous slopes of California!

But not only that; let freedom ring from Stone Mountain of Georgia!

Let freedom ring from Lookout Mountain of Tennessee!

Let freedom ring from every hill and molehill of Mississippi. From every mountainside, let freedom ring.

And when this happens, when we allow freedom to ring, when we let it ring from every village and every hamlet, from every state and every city, we will be able to speed up that day when all of God's children, black men and white men, Jews and Gentiles, Protestants and Catholics, will be able to join hands and sing in the words of the old Negro spiritual, "Free at last! free at last! Thank God Almighty, we are free at last!"

Speech 2 - President John F. Kennedy

Inaugural Address

January 20, 1961

Vice President Johnson, Mr. Speaker, Mr. Chief Justice, President Eisenhower, Vice President Nixon, President Truman, reverend clergy, fellow citizens: We observe today not a victory of party, but a celebration of freedom – symbolizing an end, as well as a beginning – signifying renewal, as well as change. For I have sworn before you and Almighty God the same solemn oath [alliteration] our forebears prescribed nearly a century and three-quarters ago.

The world is very different now. For man holds in his mortal hands the power to abolish all forms of human poverty and all forms of human life. And yet the same revolutionary beliefs for which our forebears fought are still at issue around the globe – the belief that the rights of man come not from the generosity of the state, but from the hand of God.

We dare not forget today that we are the heirs of that first revolution. Let the word go forth from this time and place, to friend and foe alike, that the torch has been passed to a new generation of Americans – born in this century, tempered by war, disciplined by a hard and bitter peace, proud of our ancient heritage, and unwilling to witness or permit the slow undoing of those human rights to which this nation has always been committed, and to which we are committed today at home and around the world. Let every nation know, whether it wishes us well or ill, that we shall pay any price, bear any burden, meet any hardship, support any friend, oppose any foe, to assure the survival and the success of liberty.

This much we pledge – and more. To those old allies whose cultural and spiritual origins we share, we pledge the loyalty of faithful friends. United there is little we cannot do in a host of cooperative ventures. Divided there is little we can do – for we dare not meet a powerful challenge at odds and split asunder.

To those new states whom we welcome to the ranks of the free, we pledge our word that one form of colonial control shall not have passed away merely to be replaced by a far more iron tyranny. We shall not always expect to find them supporting our view. But we shall always hope to find them strongly supporting their own freedom – and to remember that, in the past, those who foolishly sought power by riding the back of the tiger ended up inside.

To those [anaphora] people in the huts and villages of half the globe struggling to break the bonds of mass misery, we pledge our best efforts to help them help themselves, for whatever period is required – not because the Communists may be doing it, not because we seek their votes, but because it is right. If a free society cannot help the many who are poor, it cannot save the few who are rich.

To our sister republics south of our border, we offer a special pledge: to convert our good words into good deeds, in a new alliance for progress, to assist free men and free governments in casting off the chains of poverty [metaphor]. But this peaceful revolution of hope cannot become the prey of hostile powers. Let all our neighbors know that we shall join with them to oppose aggression or subversion anywhere in the Americas. And let every other power know that this hemisphere intends to remain the master of its own house.

To that world assembly of sovereign states, the United Nations, our last best hope in an age where the instruments of war have far outpaced the instruments of peace, we renew our pledge of support – to prevent it from becoming merely a forum for invective, to strengthen its shield of the new and the weak, and to enlarge the area in which its writ may run. Finally, to those nations who would make themselves our adversary, we offer not a pledge but a request: that both sides begin anew the quest for peace, before the dark powers of destruction unleashed by science engulf all humanity in planned or accidental self-destruction. We dare not tempt them with weakness.

For only when our arms are sufficient beyond doubt can we be certain beyond doubt that they will never be employed.

But neither can two great and powerful groups of nations take comfort from our present course – both sides overburdened by the cost of modern weapons, both rightly alarmed by the steady spread of the deadly atom, yet both racing to alter that uncertain balance of terror that stays the hand of mankind's final war.

So let us begin anew – remembering on both sides that civility is not a sign of weakness, and sincerity is always subject to proof. Let us never negotiate out of fear, but let us never fear to negotiate.

Let both sides explore what problems unite us instead of belaboring those problems which divide us. Let both sides, for the first time, formulate serious and precise proposals for the inspection and control of arms, and bring the absolute power to destroy other nations under the absolute control of all nations. Let both sides seek to invoke the wonders of science instead of its terrors. Together let us explore the stars, conquer the deserts, eradicate disease, tap the ocean depths, and encourage the arts and commerce. Let both sides unite to heed, in all corners of the earth, the command of Isaiah – to "undo the heavy burdens, and [to] let the oppressed go free."

And, if a beachhead of cooperation [anaphora] may push back the jungle of suspicion, let both sides join in creating a new endeavor – not a new balance of power, but a new world of law – where the strong are just, and the weak secure, and the peace preserved. All this will not be finished in the first one hundred days. Nor will it be finished in the first one thousand days; nor in the life of this Administration; nor even perhaps in our lifetime on this planet. But let us begin. In your hands, my fellow citizens, more than mine, will rest the final success or failure of our course. Since this country was founded, each generation of Americans has been summoned to give testimony to its national loyalty. The graves of young Americans who answered the call to service surround the globe. Now the trumpet summons us again – not as a call to bear arms, though arms we need – not as a call to battle, though embattled we are – but a call to bear the burden of a long twilight struggle, year in and year out, "rejoicing in hope; patient in tribulation," a struggle against the common enemies of man: tyranny, poverty, disease, [triad] and war itself.

Can we forge against these enemies a grand and global alliance, North and South, East and West, that can assure a more fruitful life for all mankind? Will you join in that historic effort? [hyphoroa]

In the long history of the world, only a few generations have been granted the role of defending freedom in its hour of maximum danger. I do not shrink from this responsibility – I welcome it. I do not believe that any of us would exchange places with any other people or any other generation.

The energy, the faith, the devotion [asyndetion] which we bring to this endeavor will light our country and all who serve it. And the glow from that fire can truly light the world.

And so, my fellow Americans, ask not what your country can do for you; ask what you can do for your country. [chiasmus]

My fellow citizens of the world, ask not what America will do for you, but what together we can do for the freedom of man.

Finally, whether you are citizens of America or citizens of the world, ask of us here the same high standards of strength and sacrifice [alliteration] which we ask of you.

With a good conscience our only sure reward, with history the final judge of our deeds, let us go forth to lead the land we love [alliteration], asking His blessing and His help, but knowing that here on earth God's work must truly be our own.

CHAPTER 9

THE ART OF COMMUNICATION

CHAPTER 9

THE ART OF COMMUNICATION

Small Talk is a Big Deal

Facts About Small Talk

1) No one is "really comfortable" engaging in small talk with new acquaintances (yeah... it's a bit awkward).

2) Pre-programmed questions and statements come across as, well, pre-programmed.

3) The art of small talk is NEVER about you – it's about the other person.

4) There are no rules – just guides. Setting rules makes small talk stay small.

5) Small talk is like public speaking – intimidating and it takes practice.

6) People like to talk about themselves.

7) Remember fact #6.

So… I'm uncomfortable, what do I do?

- Relax;
- Smile;
- Make eye contact;
- Say Hi;
- Introduce yourself.

Then what?

Ask questions and then follow up – no inquisitions:

"What do you think of _____?"

"What are you majoring in?"

"Have you heard of _____?"

"I really like the way you handled _____. How do you keep your cool so well?"

"Where do you go to school?" or "Where do you work?"

Remember the following:

- Observe and ask questions about what you see.
- When you are approached, remember the "Golden Rule" – treat others as you would like to be treated.
- No one-word answers.
- If you know the people you are talking to and the person approaching doesn't, introduce them.
- Keep it "comfortable" – avoid topics such as politics, religion, family, relationships, etc.
- Know when to leave or exit.

"It was great talking to you, but now I need to... "

"I'll see you at _____ in _____..."

"I have to get to a _____, thank you again..."

The "Don't" List

1) Don't think that no one is looking when you attend a networking event – someone is always looking! Picking food off a buffet with your fingers, leaving a dirty plate next to a serving tray, spitting food on the floor, picking your nose (yes, I've seen it happen more than once), etc.

2) Don't have "Paparazzi Eyes" – nothing is more insulting than someone gazing past you, as you are talking to them, to see if someone "more important" is on the way into the room.

3) Don't look at your phone or text while someone is speaking to you. Also, having a conversation while the presenter is speaking is not fair to the presenter and is disturbing to other participants.

4) Don't assume that the biggest name in the room is the one that will be most important to you.

5) Don't waste the opportunity. If a person is interesting, don't be shy – tell them so! Tell them what you enjoyed or found interesting and strike up a conversation.

Effective Meetings

"If you had to identify, in one word, the reason why the human race has not achieved and never will achieve its full potential that word would be meetings."

— Dave Barry

Meetings! We all attend them, participate in them, and to varying degrees loathe them. I'm sure you can agree that most meetings are not organized or efficient. And, they are often very time consuming and can be expensive.

One study estimated that executives spend close to half of their time (during work hours) in meetings. Numerous studies have estimated that over 10 million meetings occur each day. A University of Arizona/University of Tulsa study found that estimates of meeting expenses range from $30 million to over $100 million a year – and that's from a decade ago!

Meetings can be an organization's "silent killer" – both losing the company money and ruining morale. If an organization had a project that was continually draining the company of money, leading nowhere, and causing top employees to leave, what do you think it might do? Perhaps, get rid of it or cut the scope of it down.

I have worked with countless senior executives who have meetings practically all day long, every day. No time to work on projects. No time to return phone calls. And, barely enough time to use the facilities between meetings. When asked about when they actually find the time to do the work, the answer is always the same – at night.

When employees are in meetings all day, an organization doesn't just lose productivity, employee satisfaction, and a boatload of money – it also loses groundbreaking ideas, new concepts, and new approaches. That's because meetings can be draining and take up valuable work time.

But, as we all know, we can't just cut meetings out entirely. However, we can make them a lot more efficient and make less of them. It's like the saying, "Work smarter, not harder." Well, "Meet smarter, not more often."

Here are a few steps you can take during meetings to save your company time and money.

1) **Set an agenda** – Set a clear agenda and detail what's going to be discussed.

2) **Clear call-to-action** – What is the purpose of the meeting and what should be accomplished? What does success look like? A document? A decision? An agreement? Even if you don't achieve every objective, have clear objectives laid out in writing, and discuss where you are with each before the meeting ends.

3) **Clear expectations for every employee** – Who is responsible for what (both before the meeting begins and when it wraps up)? Who is responsible for following up on issues or calls-to-action? Make sure you articulate responsibilities out loud. Don't just assume someone knows it is his or her responsibility. Also, notate who is in charge of doing what after the meeting.

4) **Pre-meeting homework** – I have sat through hundreds of meetings at myriad organizations, and invariably a few people always come unprepared. Establishing an agenda with clear goals, defined assignments, and a clear call-to-action gets people thinking before they enter the room. In your meeting invite, you can also send a document that participants can read beforehand to get them up to speed on the meeting and how they can prepare.

5) **Hard start and end times** – Start the meeting promptly and try to avoid extraneous small talk that isn't relevant to the agenda. It's important to remember that a lack of preparation and clearly defined goals will inevitably lead to another meeting.

6) **Break the cycle** – Have two less formal meetings a week and see what happens. Give defined assignments and give people a bit more time to accomplish them, rather than just scurrying to create a last minute work product in their "free time."

7) **Film a few meetings** – It sounds tedious and you certainly don't want to film every meeting, but if you lead over 25 meetings a year, the one-hour investment of watching the tape will show you where meetings go off track and where you lose time. One taped meeting can do wonders for helping you identify ways to "meet smarter."

8) **Communication training** – If you were paying each employee by the hour (and not by salary), meetings would be a lot more concise or else! It is critical that every member of your team knows how to put together a message and deliver that message accurately, concisely, and clearly.

Time is a precious commodity. It is crucial that employees can convey and articulate concepts, arguments, and facts succinctly and quickly. Senior executives simply don't have time for an employee to take 20 minutes to explain a point that could have been made in 2 minutes.

Influencing During a Meeting

1) Determine who is who in the audience. Who is the decision maker? Who influences the decision maker?

2) What is important to the audience?

3) Develop relationships before making requests. For example: how can I help them?

4) Reposition/Repurpose – from *their* perspective.

5) Listen! What are they really saying? What is the real purpose?

6) Ask before you need to. Test your ideas out before you launch them with your audience through a Q&A.

7) Utilize past results and partnerships with that person/team.

8) Frame issues as potential opportunities rather than problems. If you identify an issue/opportunity, think about what the solution can be – this way you're bringing up an opportunity/problem and also a solution/idea.

9) Have a second (and a third) idea or solution.

10) Empathy – show that you can see yourself walking in the other person's shoes.

Communicating through Email: Rules/Etiquette

1) **Email is formal and it is final** – It lasts forever and cannot be taken back! Even if you try to recall a sent message, there is no guarantee that the person hasn't already read it. Email is the ultimate double-edged sword – it is so easy to use and feels so informal, yet it lasts forever and can always come back to haunt you.

2) **Read it back in court rule** – Don't ever think it might not happen to you. There have been plenty of cases where the prosecution or defense have used emails as admissible evidence. Before you send your email, make sure you would be happy to have it read out in court.

3) **Read it an hour or day later** – Emailing in anger is a definite no-no. Before you send it out, reread your email at a later time when you are feeling calm.

4) **Phone and talk first rule/email doesn't "emote"** – If it is important, call and talk to the person first. It is always better to discuss important things in person or over the phone.

5) **Print it out and proofread (attachments too) before sending** – It might waste paper, but will be infinitely less embarrassing than a response to an RFP loaded with misspellings!

6) **Forwarding from a business account rule** – Refer to the read it back in court rule (Rule 2).

7) **You are not just representing yourself rule** – I would advise having a personal account as well as a business account. The numbers of times people write negatives things about their boss, look for jobs, etc. – all sent from their business account – is astounding.

How to Improve Email Etiquette:

1) **Salutations and Openings** – Again, email is formal. Nine out of ten times, a formal greeting and closing is not only advisable, it is necessary. Err on the side of caution.

2) **Know Your Audience/Mirror** – You can pick up clues as to how others process information based on how they write and respond. I would pay close attention to this. I tend to try to use similar and familiar language.

3) **Subject Line** – Remember, it is not about what you are trying to communicate; it is about what your audience cares about. There is an entire art to writing subject lines that will get people to open up the email.

4) **Organize** – Again, organize your thoughts – have a message, a purpose, main points, etc. – just as you would with a formal document.

5) **Reply** – Very few things are more irritating than someone failing to reply or at least acknowledge receipt. I often ask for this when I send an email.

6) **Humor Rule** – Sarcasm and what you think is witty might not be to the receiver. Remember, your body language and non-verbal communication tools don't translate in email.

7) **Be careful with confidential information** – Refer to the read it back in court rule (Rule 2 in Rules/Etiquette).

8) **Avoid writing like a 10th grader via text** – If you wouldn't put it in a proposal or RFP response, I would try to avoid putting it in an email.

9) **Beware of the "reply all"** – Nothing has ended more careers than "Reply All."

10) **Maintain privacy/protect confidentiality** – Always err on the side of caution. If someone might not want to have his or her

email address revealed, call first. Do not put other people on the spot if you can avoid it.

11) **Your email is a reflection of you** – How would you handle yourself for a job interview, with a client, or with a superior?

The Art of Saying No – 10 Tips

1) **Depersonalize the "No"** – It's not you, it's the situation. Explain that you are following the rules, have to follow protocol, etc.

2) **Depersonalize, Part II** – Compliment them and then explain the reason you can't do it. For example, "The powers that be were so pleased with what you were able to accomplish before but we can't do what you're asking because…"

3) **Listen** – What is the person really asking for? What does the person really need?

4) **Deliver the "No"** while also delivering **at least one "Yes"** – For example, "I can't do that, but I can offer you this…"

5) **Display** that you have really thought about it and agonized over the decision.

6) **Re-frame** – For example, "I know the issue is database speed, so what if we try to…"

7) **Offer them a way to yes** – For example, "I think we might be able to accomplish that, but first I would need you to…"

8) **Try to deliver the "No" in person** – If not, then do it over an email or via phone.

9) **Don't blame** the person.

10) **Offer another alternative.**

Creating a Conversation

A speech is not a solo act – a speech is a conversation. While only one party may be speaking, all parties are communicating. Looking away, shaking one's head, raising one's brow, showing lack of interest or a face anchored in stoicism are all forms of communication – and are all part of a conversation. Smiling, nodding, clapping, cheering, and riveted attentiveness are also part of a conversation. Walking out of a conference room and doing nothing is part of the conversation too – usually the end of it.

So what can you do to ensure that a speech or presentation is in fact a productive conversation? Here are just a few ways:

1) **Involve your audience** – Do not talk at the audience; speak *with* them.

2) **Pay attention to personal pronouns** – I tend to shy away from using a lot of "I" and "me" and instead focus more on "we" and "us" as much as possible.

3) **Really involve your audience** – When I am presenting on communication or rhetoric, I occasionally involve an audience early on by asking a question addressed to one or two participants right away. I also sometimes do it in the middle of the speech. Not a confrontational question. Not a heavy question. I very rarely ask a controversial question but instead focus on a question to generate a very short response.

Here is an example: If I am giving a presentation on the need for expediency in speech, I might pick someone out and ask, "How would you feel if I told you this presentation was going to last 50 minutes? How about 5 minutes?" Or "At what point in a presentation do you start tuning the presenter out?"

It appears to be spontaneous, but it is anything but. In fact, it is a calculated move to engage the audience, raise attentiveness, and take the conversation to the next level.

Communication Tips for Technical Professionals

Having worked with technical professionals – ranging from top IT executives to Ivy League scientists to internationally ranked engineers – I fancy myself a cocktail party technologist. I understand enough about a wide spectrum of technical disciplines to discuss them for a minute or two. Just don't ask me to hook up the Wi-Fi in my own house!

The reality is that there are a lot of people like me in every organization. For example, engineers rarely work in a vacuum – there are other divisions and departments to interface with, and key business decisions are often based around communication. Can an engineer make his or her client – who is often, for example, a finance professional – understand why a change is necessary?

Here are a few tips that every engineer or technical professional can utilize to make communication with divisions, departments, and clients much easier.

1) **Pronouns** – I have been to hundreds of technical presentations in the past, and when listening to the men present, I often hear the same generic gender-specific pronoun usage (he, him, his, himself, etc.) And, as you can see, more often than not it is specific to males. Alienating any segment of your audience is never a good idea. While traditionally these have been male dominated industries, more women than ever are entering the worlds of science, technology, engineering, finance, and mathematics.

2) **Acronyms** – My rule on this is simple; unless you are CERTAIN everyone listening to you, reading your email, or receiving your document knows exactly what an acronym stands for – don't use it! Spell it out instead. I cannot state this emphatically enough!

I have witnessed countless instances when folks in one division of a particular discipline, whether IT or molecular biology, do not know what an acronym used in another division stands for. VGA might be a household term to computer wizards, but the group of financiers you are addressing won't have a clue that it means Video Graphics Array.

Assume your audience does not know and spell it out. The last thing you want is to be five minutes into your presentation and the audience is trying to figure out what the first acronym stood for.

3) **Information** – Deliver key messages right away. Especially when talking to an audience that is not made up of engineers, make sure to lay the groundwork for what they are going to be listening to so that they can follow and understand. If you are waiting to the middle or end to unleash your message, chances are the audience may already be lost. Following complex technical information is not easy for everyone.

4) **Relate** – People often understand concepts and ideas related to their own experiences. If you are explaining an engineering concept to a group of non-engineers, relate it to something the audience already understands. Analogies, metaphors, and contrasts all work – as do personal stories.

I often ask professionals to explain a concept to me as if they were addressing an eighth grade class. I find this exercise works well to help a professional prepare a presentation to an audience not well versed in engineering concepts. This often generates stories and analogies that would otherwise have remained undiscovered.

CHAPTER 10

PRESENTATION DURING AN INTERVIEW

CHAPTER 10

PRESENTATION DURING AN INTERVIEW

Interview Basics – 15 Reminders

The most important thing to remember when preparing for your interview – be yourself! In this day and age, it seems like every student has straight As, perfect test scores, and has saved millions of lives in remote lands – OK, I'm exaggerating a bit, but you get the picture. There is such strong pressure to be someone extraordinary.

However, if it's not the truth or if it's an exaggeration, you will not be able to pull it off – I promise you that. Authenticity and sincerity go a lot further than you might realize. So be true to yourself and who you are. This does not mean you need to be overly humble, but it does mean you should stay true to your character and values. Do not apologize for who you are. Be proud of who you are!

Days and Weeks Before

1) Practice interview questions and answers. Since grade school, you've probably heard that practice makes perfect. Okay, it might not make you perfect – but what is true is that practice makes you significantly better. Guess what? LeBron James

practices. Peyton Manning practices. President Barack Obama practices. Even Beyoncé practices. So before your big day, why wouldn't you practice?

2) What are your key talking points and the information you want to make sure you mention? This comes naturally with practice. Answering questions is something that we all do on a daily basis. Reflecting back on an earlier conversation and thinking, "I wish I had remembered to say..." is also commonplace. The way to prevent this is to practice answering questions ahead of time. Also, spend some time thinking about the most important things that you want someone to know about you!

3) Do your research and become very familiar with the school or organization. For example, if you are applying to a university you might say the following... "This is a great institution with great values. My father, mother, sister, brother, and grandparents all went here. I can get a great education."

What do these statements have in common?

They are the most frequent responses in college interviews and won't make you stand out! What your family has done is irrelevant – the institution wants to know about you and your specific interest in them.

Differentiate yourself – learn about the school to which you are applying, its programs, what they are known for, professors you would like to study under, groups you would like to join, etc. Make sure what you say is memorable by really researching and becoming familiar with the subject matter.

Day of the Interview

4) Dress how you wish to be perceived. What that means is, if you want to present yourself as Ivy League material, don't dress like a college dropout. Just like if you're running for president you should look presidential.

This may all sound like common sense, but it needs to be said:

shower, brush your hair, clean and trim your fingernails, iron your clothes, and shine your shoes – now that's a start. Next, make sure your socks don't have holes in them, your shoes don't look old, and your briefcase or purse isn't falling apart. Shirts should be tucked in. Clothes should match (if you aren't the most fashionable person, ask someone who is!). You do not need to look like a model, but you do need to be clean and dressed appropriately.

5) Arrive early! Ending up in the interview room drenched in sweat because you were running late is never a good idea. So unless you literally live around the corner from the location, try to arrive at least 30 minutes early to avoid surprises and allow yourself to time to focus on the task at hand.

6) Remember, as soon as you appear on location, your interview has begun. Obviously, you don't know everyone on campus. The person in the bathroom, the individual passing you in the hallway while you're on your cell phone, and the individual that you do or do not hold the door open for – could be the person interviewing you. You never know! Be careful about what you say and do while on campus. Running into your interviewer beforehand actually happens more often than you'd think.

7) Turn off your cell phone. There is nothing more distracting or rude than a cell phone going off during an interview. Vibrating is not much better. Whether it's your phone ringing or an alert that you have a new text message – make sure your phone is off. If the person interviewing you does reach for his or her phone or is texting, that is not an indication that you should as well.

Interview Time

8) Eye contact. When you meet your interviewer, look that person straight in the eye and be ready to shake hands firmly. When he or she is speaking to you, look at them. Don't dart your eyes around the room or avoid his or her glance. If a group interviews you, look at the person who is speaking to you and then

try to make eye contact with each person in the room as you respond (as long as you do not "Ping-Pong" back and forth!).

9) Smile. This one seems easy, but often isn't. When you meet someone and introduce yourself, smile. Give a genuine smile. Ask them how they are. Wait for a response.

10) Stand up straight. Watch your posture when you sit. I sound like my mother, but shoulders back and straight spine when you enter the room. Wait for your host to sit first. Once you sit, make sure your back stays straight (do not slump). Practicing with a friend or teacher before the interview can help identify how you sit under pressure. To help keep your energy up, try leaning forward about 5–10 degrees.

11) Root into your heels. Rocking back and forth, up and down, or tapping is distracting. Depending on how you sit, put your weight on one or both of your heels.

12) Listen before formulating your response. Most of us begin to formulate a response to a question before hearing the entire question. Not only does this lead to misunderstanding what is being asked, but often to speaking before the interviewer has finished! So…….

13) Remember L-P-A (Listen – Pause – Answer). The easiest way to root out disfluency (umm, ahh, like, you know) is to follow this rule. Really listen to the question and take time to process what is being asked.

Pause for a second or two before answering. This short silence shows that you are really thinking about the question. Then answer. It's always better to have a well thought out and articulate answer than a speedy one.

14) Ask at least one question yourself. There comes a time in every interview when you have an opportunity to ask questions. The interviewer may or may not ask you if you have questions. You should, regardless. This is where your research beforehand puts

you in an optimal position. Ask educated, focused, school-specific questions – it will help you stand out as a candidate.

At All Times

15) Remember your manners (please, thank you). Do not chew gum before, during, or after the interview. Always send a follow up thank you email.

20 Interview Questions You Should Master

1) Why do you want to go to this (high school, college, university)? *Or* Why do you want to work at/in _____?

2) What do you bring to this (school, position, job title)?

3) Tell me about yourself...

4) How do you plan to make a difference here?

5) What is your greatest strength?

6) What is your biggest weakness? In what area can you improve the most?

7) What accomplishment(s) are you most proud of?

8) What do you plan to do after graduation? *Or*
   What is your goal after this position?

9) Who do you look up to? Who are your role models? Why?

10) What has been the most challenging experience you have had? How did you overcome it?

11) What is your favorite subject? Why? *Or*
    What is your favorite part of your current position? Why?

12) What is your least favorite subject? Why? *Or*

What is your least favorite part of your current position? Why?

13) Tell me a story that would define who you are as a person...

14) What are your hobbies? What do you tend to do outside of school/work? Please elaborate...

15) What do you like to read outside of school/work?

What is your favorite book?

16) What teacher or mentor has had the greatest impact on you? Why?

17) If you do not get into _____, what is your plan?

18) Where else are you applying? Why?

19) If I forgot everything about you except for one thing, what would be the one thing that you would want me to remember?

20) Do you have any questions for me?

CHAPTER 11

PRESENTATIONS TO THE MEDIA

CHAPTER 11

PRESENTATIONS TO THE MEDIA

Meeting the Media – Introduction

Broadcast television. Newspapers. Magazines. Radio.

Media across the globe have adopted many practices of the Western media, running similarly styled programming, similar show formats, etc. This has created a great opportunity for you to be "ahead of the curve" in pursuing additional opportunities to represent your brand.

At the same time, the communication landscape has changed dramatically as the media landscape has changed.

The media is no longer limited to broadcast television, print and radio. Now, every person with a smartphone is a potential journalist. Every time you or your representative speak at a conference or on a panel, there is a good chance that the appearance will end up on a blog, on a website, or on a video sharing site. If there are journalists there, what once was a print interview may now actually stream onto a website.

This is NOT a reason to be nervous – it is actually a tremendous opportunity! It means a lot more potential exposure and an added opportunity for your message about the best firm in the profession to reach a much larger audience.

The key to successful interaction with the media is proper preparation.

The Camera is Never Off

The tour of your facility has ended, there were no hiccups, and now you and your "guests" are engaging in friendly banter in the parking lot. The camera (or recorder) is never off.

This media training principle not only applies to a situation when you, or your staff, are before the media.

You are the CEO of a multinational conducting a videoconference with thousands of employees. The conference has ended, but you are still in the room where the videoconference took place. The camera is never off.

You are a VP addressing 80 employees via teleconference – the phone is never off.

This mindset is not easy – the natural inclination, once the stress has subsided, the situation has turned friendly, casual conversation begins and one is no longer "on" – is to engage in conversation with those around us, and for that conversation to be less guarded. It happens to most of us (and I readily include myself).

The vast majority of the time, the camera or recorder will be off, and the phone may very well be hung up. Unless it isn't.

Whether meeting with the media, or addressing an entire company, if you adopt the mindset that the camera is still rolling, not only during the event, but before and after it, you will prevent gaffes, damaging comments, and other headaches from occurring.

If You Say It, It Will Run

Common Wisdom (Media Relations 101) – say something provocative, inflammatory, or compelling during a television taping, and it's probably going to run. Call the reporter or producer and ask him or her to pull the segment, it will *definitely* run.

Media Relations 201 – Calling a reporter after the fact and asking that the segment get pulled because you had a headache during the taping is not only a guarantee the segment will air, it also ensures that you will now have to deal with more stories (about the phone call), a much larger audience, and most importantly, it means you lose control of messaging for a period.

Three timeless tips:

1) Practice and prepare with your team before going on the air.

2) Learn about the intricacies of the media, and the outlet you are dealing with, prior to meeting.

3) If you say it, prepare to deal with it – calling the reporter after the fact and making an excuse will only draw more attention to whatever you said.

Getting from a difficult question to your answer:

- Answer the question (brevity is best);
- Transition;
- Deliver your message;
- Be comfortable in silence.

Transition Phrases (Examples):

- "Now, putting this in proper context we need to look at…"

- "Having said that…"
- "Let me put this into perspective…"
- "Let's take a look at the facts…."
- "Let's discuss the current state of the situation…"
- "The real issue here is…"
- "We asked ourselves the same thing… that is what led to…"
- "Our main concern is…"
- "What we're really talking about is…"
- "What's missing here is the issue of…"
- "To clarify…"
- "To answer, let me rephrase…"
- "More importantly…"
- "This is what I can tell you…"
- "I don't view it that way. What I (we) see is…"
- "Your question raises an even more important point…"
- "That is not an area of my expertise, but what I can tell you is…"
- "Here at…"

CHAPTER 12

CRISIS COMMUNICATION PREPARATION

CHAPTER 12

CRISIS COMMUNICATION PREPARATION

Protect Your Reputation

An unfortunate reality of life is that crises occur, and they often occur when we least expect them. Few organizations expect to be hit with a crisis on a Tuesday afternoon at 2pm when things are a bit slow and all hands are on deck, but it can happen. So what are some steps your organization can take to prepare today for a potential crisis?

1) Start planning now

Plan and prepare before you need to. What are your organizational themes when you are not in crisis mode? Identify your key messages. Who is on the messaging team? What does your organization stand for when there is no crisis? What is your organization known for? What are your organizational weaknesses?

2) Crisis response/crisis communication plan

You must have a written crisis response/communication plan. I often ask executives if their organization has a crisis response plan. The answer is almost always – "Yes." Then, I ask if they know what is in it. And, at this point the "Yes" gets a bit more sheepish. I also ask if they have reviewed it in the past six months – this is when the nervous laughter begins.

Make sure to create your plan ahead of time, review your plan regularly, amend your plan continually, and ensure that every key member of your core team is intimately familiar with the plan.

3) Assemble your direct crisis response/communication team... today!

Determine roles, chain of command, and crisis command posts –all before you need to. Trying to figure out these roles and responsibilities while you are in full crisis mode can really put the organization in a precarious position.

Who is in charge of what? Who manages the existing business? Who reaches out to customers who have yet to be affected? Who reaches out to regulators? Who contacts employees? Who reaches out to neighboring businesses? Who is in contact with the community? The media? The list goes on and on.

4) Assemble your professionals

Public relations professionals, communication specialists, industry experts, compliance professionals, public affairs professionals, outside counsel, audit teams, and crisis experts should be on auto-dial. Develop your relationships today. Identify and interview key consultants when things are quiet.

Waiting and then identifying key professionals during a crisis is much more difficult and expensive. Doing so allows for limited or no time to get them up to speed on your business and situation. It also allows for considerable time to pass and the crisis to escalate.

5) Determine internal communication protocol

Who will be responsible for communicating internally to ensure that no one is "talking outside of school?" What is the process for disseminating information throughout the organization? If you do not communicate internally, you can rest assured your employees will – and chances are you will not be happy with what they are saying and telling others.

Any person who has a touch point outside of the organization (which is everyone) has the potential to deliver a message externally that contradicts the organizational message. This usually happens because no one told that individual what was occurring or how the organization plans to respond.

6) Voice

Who is the voice of the organization? Is there more than one? Should it always be the CEO? (Answer – it depends.) How many lines of business is the company involved in? Who communicates internally? Externally? Who ensures that your business continues to operate even as the crisis develops?

7) Get your lists together

Media contacts? Adversaries? Advocates? Stakeholders? Who, outside of your organization, will speak positively about your organization in crisis? How about negatively? Who are the most crucial regulatory contacts? Trying to put these lists together in the midst of crisis never turns out well.

8) What do you say?

Do you say anything before you know anything? Failing to respond or saying "No comment" says a lot more than no comment. This is where preparedness training, drills, and live simulations really help to prepare key executives and spokespersons for the real thing.

What if there are reports of injuries? How are you receiving information? There will be a lot of incoming requests for information. How will you reach out to stakeholders?

9) Stop and breathe

Practice putting yourself into semi-stressful positions through crisis response drills. Warning – this is absolutely not a substitute and not representative of what you will feel like in the middle of a crisis.

What it does is prepare you to know how to breathe properly to control epinephrine and control your heart rate.

10) What does the filtration system look like?

In a crisis, there may be a number of parties who want answers. Who filters each call and determines who answers what? What are the answers for each?

11) Who is monitoring social and web media

What is the process for answering questions and comments online? What does the strategy look like? Whose responsibility is this? There are a number of excellent social media crisis communication professionals – having contact with one is never a bad idea. In today's day and age, ignoring the power of social media is a mistake.

12) Opposition Research

In political campaigns, not only do they research the opponent, they also research their own candidate to determine what might "pop up" at the most inopportune time.

Do a comprehensive internal "opposition research" report on

yourself – what else will come to light in the face of a crisis? What else should be on your radar screen? What are your answers?

13) Inside/outside

Do not forget to communicate internally! This point is important enough to mention twice. How you handle yourself during a crisis sends a strong message to your employees.

14) Spokesperson

Make sure your spokesperson is trained and media ready. This is one area in which on-the-job training never works! Being a spokesperson in the midst of a crisis is a brutal job to begin with. Doing so with no preparation is not only unwise, it is unfair – and will hurt your organization.

15) Pay attention to borders

If you are a multi-national organization or operate internationally, think about how a crisis abroad would affect your business here. What are your answers? Who is doing the answering?

Recent corruption allegations against major multi-nationals – that occurred thousands of miles from U.S. borders – still got a lot of media attention in the U.S.

A Crisis Doesn't Always Mean (News) Coverage

When companies communicate internally through a crisis, there is no such thing as one-size fits all approach (or one solution fits all). Every day there are myriad stories in the news about companies dealing with crisis situations; many more never make the news.

Missed earnings, resignations, down cycles, layoffs, funding issues (especially for startups), offshoring, and board shifts all have the potential to turn into major crises. And some of these have the potential to turn into very damaging internal and external crises. The damage, however, can be minimised if the organization already enjoys good relations with its investors and employees.

Relations with the Board and investors

There are clear, concrete steps every business leader can take to ensure that communication with a board or investors is much more effective during down cycles or quarters. While not a secret formula, these steps can help prevent a minor crisis from escalating in scope or an internal situation from becoming a very public external situation.

1) **Develop relationships with board members and investors BEFORE bad news or a crisis hits** – Sometimes Board members can be the best advocates a company can have during a tough quarter. However, one of the keys to having effective advocates is regular contact and flow of information, both with the Board and with investors.

   There is a reason why some of the greatest political leaders of our time continue to make phone calls and write notes to key supporters during off years – long before election season is looming on the horizon!

2) **Communicate more often** – There is a tendency (when times are good and everything is running well) to communicate a little less. This is the time to communicate more! Not only at monthly meetings – especially during tough economic times. Yes, a CEO wants to spend as much time as possible "adding value" but keeping investors and board members active, involved, and included (rather than frustrated), adds as much value as anything else.

3) **Communicate regularly** – One technique that works well is sending internal email "Updates from the CEO" consisting of a paragraph or two delivered weekly or bi-weekly with the high and low points for the company. Why? It reinforces the message of engagement with the Board and investors – by getting the

Board in the habit of receiving regular correspondence outside of when they are "supposed" to get it. This is a great initial step.

4) **Pick up the phone** – Call your investors and Board members regularly. They might be too busy to take the call. Call anyway. They may tell you that you do not need to call. Call anyway.

Relations with members of the organization

At the same time, the last thing any executive wants or can afford, is only to focus on investors and board members. Equally important is communicating regularly throughout the organization. An organization in which every member has a sense of loyalty and belonging will react much more cohesively in a crisis situation. This cohesion can be encouraged by following these communication tips:

1) **Be open, be available, talk to people** – Myriad divisions can often breed a small team atmosphere. If you are the CEO or a leader in your organization, be seen. Get out there, talk to people and, equally important, listen to people.

2) **Treat your top talent as your most precious asset** – If you think you have listened to them enough, go back and listen to them one more time. If you are not communicating with your top talent and letting them know they are heard and appreciated, they are looking elsewhere. Replacing superstars who have been headhunted is not easy.

3) **Develop a message** – Your organization needs to know not only what is going on, but what it means – the message. How does what you do, or what your team does, further the efforts of the organization? How does it help the business achieve its bottom line objectives? You MUST be able to articulate the value of your position to the organization clearly. This often takes time and effort, but is crucial – make the investment.

4) **Be Consistent** – Nothing deflates an organization or a team more than perceived inconsistency in communication or communication style.

5) **Be Open with Information** – Access to information is an essential part of morale-building within an organization. Be open with it, let people know what is going on, and allow them to feel part of the organization. This is all part of successful communication.

6) **Never try to hide the bad news** – which (a) is no longer possible and (b) will destroy all credibility. It is always better if the CEO, for example, delivers the bad news than if it is delivered by someone outside the organization.

7) **Be first** – Define the news before anyone else defines it for you. This is politics 101 – if you have negative news or news that can be construed in a negative light, communicate it first. If you don't and it exists, someone will find it. This is one game in which finishing second does not lead to a silver medal!

CHAPTER 13

TECHNOLOGY AND PRESENTATIONS

CHAPTER 13

TECHNOLOGY AND PRESENTATIONS

PowerPoint Rules

PowerPoint (PPT) has taken over the corporate universe. Since launched by Microsoft in 1990, PowerPoint (and other presentation programs since then) has become a staple in meeting and conference rooms throughout the world. An article on PowerPoint in *BusinessWeek* in 2012 disclosed that an estimated 350 PowerPoint presentations *are given each second* around the globe, 350 every second!! http://www.businessweek.com/articles/2012-08-30/death-to-powerpoint.)

When it comes to PowerPoint, there are many, many "rules" on number of slides per deck, words per slide, letters per word, etc. Most are well intentioned and many offer interesting and useful ideas. I do not believe they are all universally applicable.

I err toward brevity, both in number of slides, words per slide, etc. While not hard and fast rules, I do believe there are a number of suggestions to utilize PowerPoint effectively and efficiently. Here are a few:

1) **PowerPoint is not a presentation**. PowerPoint is a **tool** to **accentuate** or **enhance** a presentation. It is a slide deck, that's all. Not a presentation.

2) **Create an outline of your presentation** before you place it into PowerPoint (or Google Doc, or Prezi or whatever other presentation software you utilize). All too often, an executive sees a presentation "pop up" on his or her schedule, pulls up the blank PowerPoint deck, and starts plugging information into it. Resist the urge! Go through the planning process as if you were presenting without a deck. *Then* go back and accentuate your presentation with facts, figures, graphics, etc.

3) **Know your audience!** Some audiences require more detailed slides than others. Here are a few examples of actual slides. Rest assured that anyone reading the slide as you present is not focused on you and what you are saying. Not possible.

4) **Reduce the detail** – Even if you feel your audience does require more detail, remember, your audience is only human! Do not overwhelm them with detail upon detail upon detail in each and every slide. Here are examples of actual slides:

Chapter 13: Technology and Presentations

About the Template

Pitchbooks are structured presentations with tightly packed text and graphics. They are usually intended for print rather than projection. Some typical characteristics of a pitchbook presentation include:

- Smaller text sizes and more dense content layouts to enable communication of large amounts of information
- Simple graphical elements which print quickly and accurately
- High degree of consistency between slides and among sections of slides

To start creating slides using this template, click the **Home** tab, and then click **New Slide**.

Customizing the Logo

To customize this template for your business, you may want to replace our generic logo with your own.

To do this for all of your slides, switch to Slide Master View.

- On the View menu, point to Masters, and then click Slide Master.

From here, you can add your own logo. You can also customize or add additional layouts to create even more types of slides with this template.

Branding with Color

To style your slides with your company's brand colors while maintaining the template's simple layout, change the color scheme or create your own:

- On the Themes tab, under **Theme Options**, click Colors, and then select a color scheme.

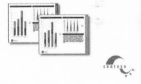

Market Risk

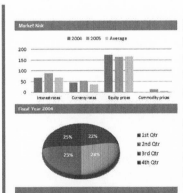

Fiscal Year 2004

Fiscal Year 2005 Annual Report

Quarter Ended	1st Qtr.	2nd Qtr.	3rd Qtr.	4th Qtr.	Total
Fiscal year 2003					
Revenue	$7,746	$8,541	$7,835	$8,065	$32,187
Gross profit	6,402	6,404	6,561	6,761	26,128
Net income	2,041	1,865	2,142	1,483	7,531
Basic earnings per share	0.19	0.17	0.2	0.14	0.7
Diluted earnings per share	0.19	0.17	0.2	0.14	0.69
Fiscal year 2004					
Revenue	$8,215	$10,153	$9,175	$9,292	$36,835
Gross profit	6,735	7,809	7,764	7,811	30,119
Net income	2,614	1,549	1,315	2,690	8,168
Basic earnings per share	0.24	0.14	0.12	0.25	0.76
Diluted earnings per share	0.24	0.14	0.12	0.25	0.75
Fiscal year 2005					
Revenue	$9,189	$10,818	$9,620	$10,161	$39,788
Gross profit	7,720	8,896	8,221	8,751	33,588
Net income	2,528	3,463	2,563	3,700	12,254
Basic earnings per share	0.23	0.32	0.24	0.34	1.13
Diluted earnings per share	0.23	0.32	0.23	0.34	1.12

(1) Includes charges totaling $750 million (pre-tax) related to the Falcidiam settlement and $1.10 billion impairment of investments.

(2) Includes stock-based compensation charges totaling $1.2 billion for the employee stock option transfer program.

(3) Includes charges totaling $756 million (pre-tax) related to Contoso subsidiaries and other matters.

The slides should accentuate and enhance the presentation – not replace it. That said, many organizations expect "pre-reads" with detailed information. If that is the case, or if your organization expects detail-laden slides, try placing the detail or "pre-reads" in the appendix, rather than having it on the screen during the actual presentation.

That affords you the ability to reference or advance to the detailed slide if you are asked, without boring or exhausting your audience if you are not.

5) **Use graphics** – Graphics, short video clips, and illustrations are very, very powerful. Illustrations can reinvigorate a tired audience. The key – make them relevant, short and powerful.

6) **But don't use space-fillers.** Use images to illustrate, not to fill space. Superfluous graphics and illustrations that do not relate to your subject matter, or add to the point you are making, only draw attention away from your message. Prepackaged designs are often disruptive or distracting.

7) **Ideas, Bullet Points, and Keywords**. Many people like to utilize slides to keep focused, almost as virtual notes. That can work effectively. Keywords or bullet points that trigger a speaker can be very helpful and beneficial. I never have more than one idea on a slide, try to limit bullet points to no more than three, and words per bullet point to four or less.

8) **Don't talk to the slide!!** If you are following along, do not speak as you look at the slide. Look at the slide, absorb the information, turn to the audience, and then speak. You do not want to project your attention, and your voice, toward the screen.

9) **Font size** is important! If your audience is straining to see, they are not focusing on what you are saying or your message. Can you see now? How about now?

10) **Limit the number of slides.** Just because everyone else uses 50 slides does not mean you have to! Just because every other

person has a slide for every last detail doesn't mean you should. Accentuate your presentation; don't replace yourself as the presenter.

Your PowerPoint Deck – Five Ways to Get it Right

Countless combined hours preparing and thousands in travel expenses, and yet it all comes down to this one moment – the pitch! Your team has worked on it in meetings, during conference calls, and over emails – reviewing, constructing, de-constructing, and tweaking the PowerPoint presentation that will determine your success... or will it?

Or maybe you are the one that is being pitched. You might have presentation commitments of your own, including justifying the expense of your department before the CFO. Or perhaps you are presenting the agency of choice to your CEO.

I can think of countless presentations that have either helped win or lose the pitch. But, PowerPoint slides are only part of a presentation. If slides were enough, there would be no reason for a presentation. You could just email the deck to the client and that would be it. So you would think that most agencies and in-house practitioners spend as much time practicing the delivery of the presentation as they do preparing the slides, right?

We all know what usually happens. Endless hours are spent putting the deck together, making changes to it up until an hour before the pitch – sometimes even right before. Then there is travel to the presentation site, overcoming jetlag, getting the team together to regroup, and maybe getting a chance to practice a few minutes before entering the boardroom. You might have scheduled a conference call before the presentation to discuss roles, who will address what, and who is responsible for different lines of questioning. In the end, the scale of balance between preparing the deck and practicing the presentation is skewed dramatically.

A well-delivered presentation with only a few or even no slides will always succeed over a poorly delivered presentation with superior slides. Again, if slides were enough, you would not need to present.

When it comes to a presentation, you have to ask yourself the following questions. How does the team gel? How do individual team members answer questions? How are transitions handled? Who do team members look to when they are unsure? Who is uncomfortable presenting? What personality traits may turn off an audience member? How succinct is each team member? Who reviewed this only a few minutes before coming in and is woefully unprepared? Who disengages when others speak?

These are all questions that will never be answered by a slide deck. These questions and countless others like them are the reason you are presenting in person rather than just emailing your presentation to the client.

Delivery matters as much as content – and preparation should reflect that.

So how do you prepare when time is limited, the client demands a thorough deck, and team members are spread all over the place? Here are a few suggestions:

1) **Narrate as You Create** – When preparing slides (even the first iteration), determine who will be delivering it. That person MUST have input into the creation of the slide. Watching someone deliver information of which he or she has no ownership is painful and obvious.

2) **Live is Better** – Try to get together to practice for a few hours in the weeks, days, and evenings prior to the presentation. You will see things in person that need tweaking that you will never notice over a live conference call or video. These small adjustments can have a huge impact.

3) **If Live Isn't an Option then Utilize Technology** – Skype, while not optimal, allows you to practice individual parts of your presentation live. You can also tape the call and then watch it later to help critique each other.

4) **The Evening Before** – Every team member needs to be in sync before a critical presentation. It's a good idea to get everyone together the night before to review the presentation and get comfortable. If even one team member arrives late to the meeting or forgets something important it can cause the entire group to fall out of sync.

5) **Practice Saves Time** – You will have extraneous information in your deck that you won't realize without practice. But, your audience will. Practice your presentation and trim out the superfluous information. It'll end up saving you time.

When Technology Comes to Work – 11 Tips

There are great articles in *The New York Times, Forbes,* and *Entrepreneur* on the potential pitfalls to avoid when meshing out newfound mobility with face-to-face interactions in the workplace.

While this is not a definitive guide by any means, these 11 tips will help you safely navigate the new workplace and avoid undesirable situations:

1) **Smartphones are not always associated with work** – Justly or unjustly, tablets and Smartphones are often associated with activities such as texting, games, and other non-work activities (unlike laptops). Be aware of that when you pull one out during a meeting.

2) **Tell us!** – Many people (including myself) like to take notes digitally. If you do pull out a Smartphone or tablet during a meeting to take notes, make sure to tell other attendees, "I use my iPad to take notes." This will prevent others from wondering if you are

checking Facebook or playing Candy Crush.

3) **Social media** – Many companies have a social media policy. In fact, every organization should! That said – if you have work friends that use social media, they may realize you were actually using your Smartphone or iPad to tweet or post something to Facebook during a meeting. Don't assume your content or the time you posted it will remain a secret. Be cognizant of what you post and when you post it during work hours.

4) **Laptops** – I often present in corporate conference rooms and will see eight or more people whip out their laptops to take notes. At a medium sized conference table that is a lot of laptops and not a lot of space. Imagine 13"–17" barriers between the presenter and the audience. This is one area in which I think tablets are actually more effective.

5) **Set rules** – If it is your meeting, set the rules. Ask people to set their phones to silent or turn them off. Asking people not to take notes digitally is a stretch, but you can ask them not to check their email during the meeting.

6) **Discretion** – Some things are unavoidable – important phone calls and emails. What is avoidable though is a lack of communication around those. If you are expecting a critical call, tell everyone about it before the meeting starts so there is no confusion if you need to excuse yourself.

7) **Keep email in its place!** – Constantly checking your email on your Smartphone or tablet in front of colleagues and clients, sends a message that you don't want to send. Again, if you are awaiting a crucial or time-sensitive email, let people know. If you think you are multi-tasking by speaking to a colleague and typing away, you are incorrect. Your colleague may never say anything, but you can be sure they find it rude; it sends the message that the text or email is more important than they are.

8) **Email does not emote!** – Emails are rarely seen as being too

soft. Emails have no intonation, emotion, tone, gestures, or facial experiences. Remember that! Reread your emails before you send them, and if there is even the slightest chance that your email might be misinterpreted, rewrite it or pick up the phone instead. Reread "Communicating through Email: Rules/Etiquette" in Chapter 9.

9) **Context** – The other place where email often misses the mark and causes hurt feelings is context. You send a well thought out, well-constructed email to a colleague. The response is "Fine." The sender then wonders why he/she received a curt, short email. The responder on the other hand doesn't even give it another thought as he or she may just have landed, is going through 100 emails, or wanted to reply quickly and get back to work. Without context provided, context can often be assumed or invented. That never turns out well. Think about the context of your emails and how they will be interpreted when writing them.

10) **Remote team members** – If you have a team in which most employees work on site, but one team member works remotely – that team member is at a disadvantage. There is a certain camaraderie that forms just from working with people hours and hours each day. In addition, there might be some jealousy around the person that gets to work from home or remotely. Make a real effort to ensure that remote team members are on site a few times per year to interact face-to-face with colleagues. Videoconferences will not replace in person interactions.

11) **Attention!** – Always remember that when someone is talking to you, do not look at your Smartphone or laptop. We are all guilty of it – listening to someone, while typing or reading an email. Give the person in front of you your full attention. It matters! Trust me – people have lost jobs and important projects because of this.

Five Teleprompter Tips

The teleprompter has gotten quite a bit of attention recently. After witnessing many *faux pas*, here are my five quick tips to make the teleprompter experience a bit more rewarding for you.

1) Always bring a physical copy of the text with you: there is nothing worse than discovering that the text you thought was loaded into the teleprompter was loaded incorrectly or is not working. Remember that with any electronic device it can fail to work properly.

2) Tennis is best left on the court: it is often obvious when a speaker is using a teleprompter as the speaker's head tends to turn from left to right, as if watching a tennis match – moving from screen to screen.

3) Create your own teleprompter "lingo": This would be a type of shorthand – whether phonetic spelling, underlining, "stressors", hyphenated pauses, etc. – inserted into the text to remind you when to pause, change your tone, lighten the atmosphere, use a natural gesture etc. It is easy to lose the connection with the audience while using a teleprompter by speaking in a monotone voice with no intonation or expression.

4) Don't stare! – If you are using a single screen teleprompter (especially if using it to record a presentation to be viewed later) remember you are talking to people, not to the machine! While eye contact is crucial, there is a fine line between constant eye contact and staring. If you are not making eye contact at all, it becomes obvious you are reading. Break your visual contact, even for a second or two.

5) Practice. Practice. Practice. – If you are going to use a teleprompter, practice extensively with it every time. Just because you are comfortable with it for one address does not mean you will be as comfortable the next time. Also, familiarity with the text is critical to success when using this device.

CHAPTER 14

ACADEMIC PRESENTATIONS

CHAPTER 14

ACADEMIC PRESENTATIONS

Connecting with your Class: A Guide for Educators

For tens of thousands of students, the new semester and school year begin every September and January.

Many professors and teachers will be speaking to a rapt classroom with eager students who are consumed with enthusiasm for the subject matter. Unfortunately, some professors will be teaching classes where establishing a connection with the class is as difficult as finding the proverbial "needle in a haystack."

You might be lecturing in a required course, and more students are in attendance because they *have* to be there than because they *want* to be there. You might be in an intro level class with so many students that you are having a hard time connecting with any of them.

Maybe you are teaching a difficult technical class to a not interested or intimidated audience, or teaching a required class to an audience that is interested in something else.

For corporate presenters, your first class can occur at any point in time – a new division is started, two departments are merged, or you are tasked with teaching people, with whom you have never previously interacted, something that is crucial to the company, and to your career.

Fear not.

There are steps every professor can take to connect with students while teaching. Many of these steps will help to put a nervous or anxious professor at ease as well.

The key is to establish that connection as soon as possible, and the first class is the best opportunity to do so. As the semester or school year continues you will connect with individual students who come to office hours, show interest or participate; the first classes are your opportunity to connect with most of your students, and engage them immediately.

Here are 10 steps for Day 1:

1) Smile – When your students first start to arrive in your classroom, they will be looking for you to set some sort of tone. Set the tone with a warm face and genuine smile. If you don't appear interested in teaching the class, why would a student be excited about taking it?

2) Why You - You might be teaching the class because you want to or you might be teaching the class because it was assigned to you. Determine what about the information you are going to be teaching matters to you, why it matters, and why your students should care. One idea is to answer the following question. "What is the most valuable piece of advice you can provide for your students to help them succeed, based on your experiences as a student in this subject area?" Stories that humanize you are helpful as well. Allowing students to see another dimension to

you, rather than just the label of "Professor _____" will help to establish a connection.

3) Introduce yourself – Share your background and rather than just providing an abbreviated C.V., tell your students why you are teaching this class, why you care about the subject matter, and why you studied this subject.

4) Ask students to introduce themselves – It is a great way to break the ice, develop some collegiality among your students, and give you a better idea of who you are teaching. This allows you to determine how this class will not only help students reach a requirement, but also benefit those same students as they pursue individual majors and specific learning interests.

In a large class this becomes extremely difficult, but still possible. One idea - This is going to sound a little strange, but ask each student to introduce herself or himself to the person seated the right and the left. While this will not directly help you learn more about your students, it will at least generate some conversation among students, and may result in increased collegiality.

One more way to try to lower the barrier in a large class is, literally, to step away from the lectern, walk to the front row, and introduce yourself to a student. Ask the student a basic question about his or her experience with the subject matter, and then use this as an opportunity to pivot and ask the class, "How many other people feel the way that _____ does?" You can now continue to ask further questions to learn more and, really, to build up a relationship with the students. The trick here is to ask questions that are fairly benign, avoid being confrontational, and thank each student who speaks up.

5) Why this class? – "Because I had to" is not the reason that you want students to provide at the end of the semester if asked why they took your class. Take control of the situation and define why this class is important at the outset. How do you do this? Get an idea of who your students are, and how the information you impart will help them.

One example: "Biology impacts every facet of our lives, and can make you a better scientist, executive or poet. Over the course of this semester I will show you how."

Another example: "Over the course of the next 12 weeks, we will learn how _____(subject name) impacts every person and every student, whether you are majoring in art history, zoology, or any subject in-between."

6) Support your students – A nice signal to send students on Day 1 is that you are going to be there to support them. The class might be very difficult, and you can tell your students that. There might be quite a bit of homework. You can tell them that. Just don't tell them that you have office hours in the same tone, or vein, that an attorney would provide rules at a deposition.

An example: "This class will be difficult, but I will be here to support you every step of the way. I can make you this promise – if you try your hardest, schedule time with me when you have difficulty, go to T.A. Hours, etc., you will do ok in this class." (Hint: this only works if that is true!)

7) Show them – If you are assigning homework over the first few classes, ask for a student volunteer, or pick a student. Then surprise them by taking one of the homework problems or questions and actually showing them, step by step, how you would gather the information, utilize said information and approach the answer. Literally step by step. This may be similar to when you were a young student taking this course material for the first time.

This may seem cumbersome, and it is. It also shows your students you are in it with them. You meant it when you said it. It is crucial that you don't leave a student at the board struggling when doing this – you are taking them through your thought process, step by step. This will help them, and will help you.

8) Fun – Incorporate something fun into your first lecture. Not necessarily funny, but fun. A video. A story. An anecdote. A light moment will not distract your students; it will actually

re-focus them. It will also show them you are (a) human and (b) have interests other than your subject area, and grading them in that subject area.

9) Current Events – One way to make the first class more interesting is to scan your favorite newspaper or current events website, and connect the subject you are teaching to something happening in the news. One way to do this successfully is by connecting your class subject with a current event or current "hot" topic a student would not typically associate with your subject area.

10) An example – "Last night was (pick an event.) Well (sporting event), at first glance, has absolutely nothing to do with (pick a subject). But in reality, it does have something to do with (subject). What we will learn over the next few weeks is how (subject) affects many areas of our lives...."

Learn from hosts – This may not be appropriate for every class, but I find that this works to establish connection with any audience. It has the added benefit of putting a nervous professor at ease. Greet students as they enter your classroom.

"Hi, I'm Dr. _____, it is a pleasure to meet you."

This changes the mood in the classroom immediately, as now you are no longer speaking to a room full of strangers.

While these are by no means the only ways to connect with students, they offer a strong start. Remember, the class is not about you. It is about your audience, and it is easier to educate once you have made a connection.

The Best Defense – Defending your Dissertation

For many students, the approaching winter season means focusing on final exams, maybe graduation, and then a well-earned winter break. For those pursuing an advanced degree, the semester break won't come. Preparing for a dissertation or thesis continues 365 days a year, many of those days seeming to approach the 24-hour mark.

We have worked with students preparing to present research, defend a thesis, or defend a dissertation, and have spoken to myriad students about their experiences. What we have learned is that there are some key lessons a student can take from other disciplines when preparing to defend a dissertation or thesis. Here are six:

1) **Defend, But Don't Be Defensive**. Whether running for office, appearing on "60 Minutes" or appearing before your dissertation/thesis committee, appearing defensive never works. Remember, defensiveness often appears not in the language used, but in the delivery – slight frowns; quick, heated responses; flushed face; impatient tone – all appear defensive, and stay with the person across the table (or screen) for a long time. Keep cool by mastering breathing techniques and techniques to depersonalize questions.

2) **Research Your Research**. When running for office, any candidate worth his or her salt not only conducts research on the opponent, but also on himself/herself. It is far better to know pain points, and be able to prepare for them, then to get "caught cold" in an interview or during a debate. The same holds true for defending your dissertation or thesis. Determine the questions that upset, annoy, or concern you the most about the research you will present. To the extent possible, address likely questions or any controversial topics upfront in your presentation. Prepare to answer them, and practice those answers.

3) **Dissertation Day Shouldn't Be Day One**. Skilled debaters do not jump into a debate with no practice. Great orators practice great speeches – no one knew that more than Winston Churchill, who, when preparing an address, reportedly practiced for one hour for every one minute of a speech. Rehearsing the presentation of your dissertation/thesis, as well as conducting practice defenses, can work. Rehearsing can occur independently, with loved ones or with colleagues. Practicing defenses with

colleagues can be very beneficial, as not only do you get the experience of live Q&A, you also have an opportunity to work through answers, find holes in your presentation, and often find more effective ways to present some of your research and ideas.

4) **LPR – Listen, Pause, Respond.** O.K., obviously it is never that simple. However, when fielding questions from your committee, responding instantly often indicates that you did not listen to the entire question, as the formulation of a response takes, at a minimum, a second or two. Watch any interview on television – often, the interviewee misses the intent of the question as the response was being formulated before the interviewer finished speaking. Listen to the question – really listen to the question – and give yourself a few seconds to formulate your response and determine what you really want to say. Everyone will appreciate it, chances of mistakes are minimized, and the precious few seconds that feel like forever to you feel like a few fleeting seconds to those who asked the questions.

5) **You Are the Expert!** You put years into researching, writing and preparing. You should know at least as much about your material as everyone else in the room – approach this less like a defense and more like a presentation of exciting research that everyone will want to know about. Remember that every person in the room has gone through the process, and chances are you will be on the other side of the conversation at some point. To reach this point you must have confidence in your findings – make sure you project that confidence when you present.

6) **Clarification, please.** It is the nightmare scenario – a poorly worded answer or misstatement resonates through the committee and builds into a heated debate between the entire committee and the candidate. This is where there is tremendous value in knowing each committee member's school of thought, personality, conversational style, and how that might work in a group dynamic. This is no different from if you were being interviewed on a particular television program. If you sense an answer was

not received the way you intended, clarify your answer immediately. This is also another reason to give yourself a second or two after a question is asked before you respond, to make sure you know not only what you want to say, but how you want to say it.

Communication Tips for Entrepreneurs

Breaking news—if you are a startup pursuing funding, you have more in common with a politician or athlete caught behaving badly than you might think.

What do a politician caught misbehaving, an athlete photographed doing something inappropriate, or a celebrity with a heated moment caught on tape have in common? They all have the ability to control how they respond to the situation. How they communicate will likely determine whether the incident is a minor bump in the road or a career ender.

So what does this have to do with entrepreneurs pursuing Venture Capital (VC) funding? Everything!

Crisis communication is usually identified as the effort to protect and defend the reputation of an individual, organization or corporation when crises strike and public confidence in the individual or organization is shaken or thrown into question.

Entrepreneurs often face the same situation every day while trying to raise capital. The crisis is always the same – a lack of funding puts the entire startup in danger. Without funding or an operating budget, key personnel will pack up and head for greener pastures. This leaves a startup in a lot of trouble (to say the least). So what is the startup to do? Pitch (communicate with) Venture Capitalists to raise the capital to end the crisis!

Lessons for Entrepreneurs:

1) **Have a Central Message** – The images are very clear...the "repentant" politician standing at the dais, wife at this side, as he

stumbles through a very awkward and very long-winded statement that says twenty different things, which means he has said – Nothing!

The value of having a message cannot be overstated. If you are pursuing funding, you must be able to identify how you will deliver a return on that investment, profits, and you must be able to do this in a manner that is clear, consistent, and easy to comprehend. Remember, you are asking people to invest at a time when investing, no matter the size of the VC firm, is a scary thing to do.

Why should the VC invest in your company? The risk to the VC is obvious but the potential reward may or may not be. What mitigates that risk and gets the company across the finish line?

2) **It is not about YOU – The athlete accused of using banned substances often forg**ets that it is not about him – it is about the fan that has placed his or her trust in the athlete and now feels betrayed. The point of view the athlete takes often determines whether he is forgiven or the loyalty is gone forever.

As much as your pitch may be about your company, it really isn't – it is about the VC that you're pitching to, his or her investment, and what that investment in your company will mean to the VC in terms of opportunity cost, time, energy, effort, and ultimately the Return on Investment.

3) **Be Open** – Like investigative reporters, VCs are (usually) very adept at plying their trade, and that means that when a crisis strikes (or you need funding), just like the reporter, the VC will probably know what the hot button issues are and where to look.

Be transparent – hiding information, trying to gloss over or bury a problem will do more harm than good. If there is bad news, it will get out – so get it out on your terms. What you don't say often speaks volumes.

4) **Body Language Matters** – An apology given with a smirk or done with arms crossed and a hostile look (don't laugh, I've seen

it) is always recognized, and the result is never good.

In that same vein, looking down during a pitch, speaking toward your shoes, hands in your pockets, fidgeting, bouncing back and forth on each foot (very common) always sends a message. Is body language the major difference maker for a pitch? Not necessarily. Does it matter? Yes, because it sends a message.

5) **Words Matter** – When a major crisis strikes a Fortune 50 company, every word uttered by the CEO and/or spokesperson is analyzed. The choice of words, the tone and terminology is a potential landmine. Each element could lead to a devastating blow. When pitching a VC, put thought into what you say. After all, you are asking for millions of dollars. Don't you think your word choice matters? (Hint: the answer is yes!)

6) **Practice and Prepare** – I cannot overstate the importance of practicing and preparing. The road of busted startups is littered with great ideas and great leaders who failed to prepare for the pitch and didn't receive the funding.

7) **Every "Crisis" is an Opportunity** – Every crisis provides an opportunity for a leader to show his or her true colors. This is often a turning point where a leader can gain popularity or sink, depending on how a crisis is handled. Every pitch affords an entrepreneur the same opportunity.

CHAPTER 15

POLITICAL COMMUNICATION

CHAPTER 15

POLITICAL COMMUNICATION

Debate Prep 101

Political campaigns spend an inordinate amount of time raising money to do one thing – deliver their message to the voters, most often through paid media. Precious positive "earned" media opportunities – stories involving a candidate in a positive light, in print or on television –become like rainbows without rain – very rare.

Debates are not limited to politicians. Most of us engage in healthy debate regularly.

Ten tips for success in debates

Debates are a very rare opportunity for political candidates to get over an hour of free – FREE – exposure before the electorate. Almost all races (State, Senate, Congress) have locally televised debates, and bigger races get the opportunity to debate on much bigger stages – venues such as "Meet the Press," etc. These opportunities can offer an underfinanced candidate an all-star performance, which usually leads to multiple days, or even weeks, of positive "earned" media exposure to follow. Yet, many candidates spend more time preparing breakfast than preparing for a debate, and it shows.

Which brings us to Debate Prep 101: Top 10 Tips for Success."

1) **If you don't prepare**, you know how you will fare! (Hint: not well!)

2) **Too Long is Wrong** – The moment is finally here...the moderator has offered up a softball, "Candidate xyz, how do you feel about ____?" This is the ultimate opportunity to really deliver a crisp, focused, and moving message. The candidate answers and hits a home run, and then...keeps going, and going, and going, until finally the moderator puts a painful end to it.

3) **Never Forget...to Memorize** - Governor Jan Brewer of Arizona was the victim of trying to memorize an opening statement, and... she blanked. It happens to everyone, but very rarely on such a national stage. Audiences will forgive a lot, but an audience will not forgive blanking on an opening statement when you must articulate why you are running for office. More on Governor Brewer's tough week to follow...

4) **Bills Don't Pay** – I have trained dozens of incumbents, and most share one trait when it comes to answering a debate question. "My bill on..."; "Senate Bill 1234, which I co-sponsored...;" House Resolution 123, which I voted against... ." Other than very contentious, very public pieces of legislation, the public rarely remembers a bill number and even in that circumstance, talk about the issue behind the bill, not the bill itself. Hint: When unemployment and taxes are through the roof, not too many people will believe that your bill, regardless of party affiliation, will change everything instantly.

5) **Smile!** You're on Candid Camera! – Today, if you are running for dogcatcher and are debating, someone will be recording it. If you err, say something questionable or gaffe, it will be on YouTube. Approach your opponent before the debate begins,

smile, shake hands, and act like an adult for the next hour. Even if the debate isn't televised, if you mess up, it will be.

6) **Be a Composer** – Your delivery is as important as your content. Allow your cadence to guide the listener. Allow your tone to serve as a verbal highlighter when you are making a point, changing course, or framing an issue. Pause between thoughts. Your voice is an instrument. If you are making a dramatic point, build up to it through changes in tone.

7) **Don't Lose Your Composure** – I have yet to see a candidate lose a debate solely for being too civil. I have seen many lose solely by failing to be civil enough.

8) **Mind Your Manners** – No pointing, slouching, smirking, scowling – all send a message, and all have led to debate losses by major party candidates in the past two decades.

9) **Fighting is for Fools** – Debates are not the time for anger, invective, or cursing, etc. A debate is a duel, not a fight, and there is a difference.

10) **Discipline Defeats Drama** – A disciplined candidate has a message, stays on the message, maintains decorum and directs the line of discussion, as opposed to reacting constantly to an opponent. Discipline trumps drama every time.

AUTHOR BIOGRAPHY

AUTHOR BIOGRAPHY

Matt Eventoff, owner of Princeton Public Speaking, is an internationally recognized communication and messaging strategist.

He regularly works with junior, senior, and C-level executives in organizations ranging in size from startups to Fortune 500 companies. He has worked with leading multinational organizations, the U.S. Department of State, YPO-WPO (Young Presidents' Organization), Ivy League professors, authors, professional athletes, entertainers, public figures, and leaders from myriad other industries. He has trained clients throughout the United States, Central America, the Middle East, Africa, Europe, and Asia.

Matt's specialties include communication training, message development training, and communication strategy. He has successfully prepared clients to appear before almost every audience and on nearly every network and major cable news program, including *60 Minutes, 20/20, Nightline, Dateline, Frontline, Hardball,* and *Good Morning America.*

He is a frequent lecturer on crisis communication, public speaking, interacting with the media, legal communication, and messaging at colleges and universities – including undergraduate and graduate programs at Princeton University, the University of Pennsylvania, Notre Dame, University of Maryland, Rutgers University, Ohio State

University, University of Colorado Boulder, Academy of Science in Kiev – Ukraine, Doshisha University in Kyoto – Japan, and many other institutions.

Matt is frequently cited by leading publications and news outlets on issues related to communication, including *The New York Times, USA Today, Forbes, CNBC, NPR, BusinessWeek, ABC News, Bloomberg, The AP (Associated Press), BBC,* and *The Washington Post.*

Matt serves as professional advisor to the Princeton University student organization Speak with Style. Matt received his Bachelor's degree from the University of Maryland and his Master's degree from the University of Pennsylvania.

Made in the USA
Charleston, SC
24 March 2014